THE MOUNTAIN

THE RI

THE MOUNTAIN BIKER'S GUIDE TO

THE
RIDGEWAY

Andy Bull and Frank Barrett

STANLEY PAUL

LONDON   SYDNEY   AUCKLAND   JOHANNESBURG

Stanley Paul & Co. Ltd
An imprint of the Random Century Group

20 Vauxhall Bridge Road
London SW1V 2SA

Random Century Australia (Pty) Ltd
20 Alfred Street, Milsons Point, Sydney, NSW 2061

Random Century New Zealand Limited
191 Archers Road, PO Box 40–086, Auckland 10

Century Hutchinson South Africa (Pty) Ltd
PO Box 337, Bergvlei 2012, South Africa

First published 1991

Set in Plantin by 📐 Tek Art Ltd,
Addiscombe, Croydon, Surrey

Printed and bound in Great Britain by
Martins of Berwick

A CiP catalogue record for this title is available
upon request from the British Library

ISBN 0 09 174644 2

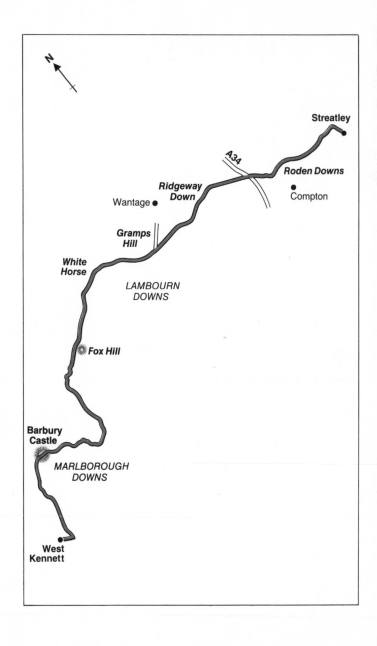

CONTENTS

About the book   8

Preface   10

Introduction   12

chapter 1   WEST KENNETT to BARBURY CASTLE   23

chapter 2   BARBURY CASTLE to FOX HILL   32

chapter 3   FOX HILL to THE WHITE HORSE   42

chapter 4   THE WHITE HORSE to GRAMPS HILL   51

chapter 5   GRAMPS HILL to RIDGEWAY DOWN   60

chapter 6   RIDGEWAY DOWN to THE A34   70

chapter 7   THE A34 to RODEN DOWNS   77

chapter 8   RODEN DOWNS to STREATLEY   87

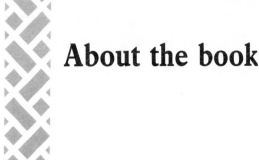

About the book

There are a number of cycling books on the market which can tell you all about hub/gear ratios, freewheel sprockets and side-pull brakes. This isn't one of those books.

We're not expert mountain bikers in the normal sense: we couldn't tell you how to adjust your gears – we're not even much use at mending punctures.

Our only qualification for writing this book is that we like mountain biking. Not using a mountain bike to nip down to the newsagent to pick up an evening paper; or simply to indulge in a bit of posing. We enjoy putting a mountain bike to the use for which it was originally intended.

This guide concentrates on the Ridgeway – but it is as much a guide to the pleasures of mountain biking as it is to the sights and scenery you will encounter en route.

The main part of the book is divided into chapters which tackle the Ridgeway section by section. You don't have to try to conquer the whole route in one go – although this is perfectly feasible if you start early enough and have the stamina. As well as listing the main sights and historical attractions en route – with information on some of the famous people connected with that region – we also suggest some other rides in the same area. The Ridgeway is at the centre of a whole network of paths and tracks that criss-cross the Downs – the choice of alternative routes and circuits is practically limitless. With an Ordnance Survey map and some imagination you could cycle off-road for weeks and never cover the same ground twice.

Each section also contains valuable service information about hotels, pubs, shops and cycle stores.

We have tackled the Ridgeway from west to east, starting in Wiltshire, in the belief that the wind should normally be at your back (though the British weather is never predictable). If you want to use the book back to front, there is no reason why you shouldn't work east to west.

Whichever way you go, one thing is certain – you are sure to enjoy yourself. If you have a mountain bike, and have never used it off-road, this book will offer you a good introduction.

We hope you have fun.

If you have comments on or suggestions for the book, please write to us at Ridgeway Mountain Bike Book, PO Box 67, Bath, Avon.

Frank Barrett
Andy Bull

Preface

It's not exactly an exhaustive survey of public opinion, but the British Rail guard who helped us load a bike on to a train at Paddington station probably summed up many people's feelings on the subject.

"That's an impressive-looking piece of expensive machinery," he said, and added sarcastically: "Twenty-one gears? Light-weight frame? I expect you go up a lot of mountains on that, don't you? I don't expect you go on it further than the pub."

It was a fair observation. Many people, including many who buy them, see mountain bikes as a sort of fashion accessory – "high street jewellery" to use one description. It looks good, it's expensive – and, almost as an afterthought, it's a useful means of transport around town.

Probably as many as half of the new bikes that are bought in Britain are mountain bikes – that's a million a year, a remarkable figure when you consider they have been available in this country for less than ten years.

Like most modern trends, mountain biking came out of America. About 15 years ago in Marin County, California, a bunch of post-hippy bike freaks developed a passion for riding down mountains on old-fashioned American bikes with balloon tyres. These lunatic races became popular and quickly attracted the attention of bike manufacturers – particularly the Japanese, who know a good thing when they see one.

From these early prototype machines, the mountain bike was born. It has rapidly become the most lucrative part of the retail bike trade and the mainstay of the city cycle messenger service business. But few mountain bike owners actually use their expensive, elegant machines to venture off the beaten track.

This is a great pity. The truth is that mountain bikes perform to their best ability off the metalled road (enthusiasts for conventional bikes dislike the heavy, energy-absorbing tyres of mountain bikes). A mountain bike only really comes into its own in the countryside – riding up a rough lane, where you have a chance to work through the whole range of gears. A mountain bike offers a unique chance to see the best of the British countryside.

But the idea of such "serious" mountain biking probably strikes the casual cyclist as a little too daunting. In fact "serious" mountain bikers in their cut-off trousers and crash helmets, with their trade talk of braised fillets and oversize headsets, don't look much like people keen to enjoy themselves. And mountain bikes appear to eschew the benefits of mudguards – "serious" mountain bikers seem to want to get wet and muddy.

Don't be put off. Part of the reason why we decided to write this series of mountain bike guides is to show that the whole business can be fun. To get the most pleasure out of mountain biking, you don't need mountains – although mountains can be fun. All you need is to find a route away from the main highways.

This isn't as difficult as you might think. The whole of Britain is criss-crossed with a huge network of tracks and paths, particularly bridleways, over which mountain bikes can be taken. Within an hour's drive of Charing Cross, for example, you can dump the car, hop on a mountain bike and find yourself deep in the heart of the wildest countryside.

You don't necessarily need cut-off shorts, or even a crash helmet – though you may find both more useful than you think. What you need is a sense of adventure and plenty of energy and enthusiasm.

But be warned: what starts as a pleasant pastime can quickly become a habit-forming obsession. After a few expeditions, you could soon find yourself at the bike shop drooling over light-weight frames and lasciviously eyeing the latest accessories. It's worth the risk . . .

Introduction

Imagine that you are travelling east along the Ridgeway from Ogbourne St George. Just before the small hamlet of Fox Hill, with its cheerful pub The Shepherd's Rest, you reach the point where the Ridgeway crosses the M4 motorway. After perhaps a good ride of some five or six miles during which you have crossed one of the emptiest – but still one of the most lovely – stretches of countryside in southern England, you descend a rough track. And here, on this bridge over the motorway, you abruptly come face to face with the twentieth century.

A short while before, you were probably standing on Liddington Hill, the highest point of the downs: looking east and west, the Ridgeway can be seen threading its way in either direction. It's almost impossible to stop your eye following the path to its vanishing-point on the horizon – up here there is nothing to obscure the view: no buildings, few trees, never a car and hardly ever many people.

England is said to be one of the most overcrowded countries in Western Europe, but looking around from this high vantage point it's easy to believe that you are alone in the world: apart from the cry of a skylark or the far-off bleating of a sheep, there are few signs of life.

Standing up on Liddington Hill, once an Iron Age fort, it's easy to think you're on the very top of the world. Like the small boy in *The Snowman*, you can almost imagine that all you have to do is to stretch out your arms and you would be lifted up into the clouds. All along the Ridgeway, the sky seems to wash over you like water.

But at this point, if you can't see it yet, you can certainly hear the motorway; at first, it sounds almost like the distant rush of the sea. (It's one of the curiosities of the Ridgeway that at many stretches of the path you turn a corner and half expect to glimpse the sea spread out before you.)

Even the motorway, however, can do nothing to spoil the feeling of content and fascination generated by travelling the Ridgeway. In fact, as you pause on the bridge and watch the apparently endless succession of heavy lorries and coaches labouring up the hill towards you, it's impossible not to reflect on history.

The M4 motorway was mostly completed in the early 1970s. No one is exactly sure when the Ridgeway was first in use; according to the best guess, it was certainly in existence by the year 2000 BC. Will the M4 last for 4,000 years? It seems unlikely. (And one doubts whether archaeologists of the future will feel the need to ponder over the significance of what remains of our service stations or emergency telephones, in the way that we seek clues to explain the ancient history of the Ridgeway and to identify the peoples who used it in its earliest days.)

The Ridgeway is often called the "oldest road in Europe"; it's a claim that is difficult to contradict. It seems extraordinary that the Ridgeway was already 2,000 years old by the time that the Romans invaded Britain. Perhaps even more extraordinary is that it has been in continuous use as an important highway for almost the whole of its life. Only since the early part of this century, with the coming of metalled roads and the rise of the motor car, has the Ridgeway fallen into comparative disuse.

To the north of the route, at many points you can glimpse the main-line railway from Bristol to London, Paddington – Brunel's famous "billiard table" GWR – God's Wonderful Railway, as the Great Western Railway used affectionately to be known. To the south of the Ridgeway runs the A4 road, one of the great highways of England – the old Great West Road which once carried stage-coaches from Bristol to London. Before the opening of the M4, this was one of the busiest roads in England – now for much of its length it has reverted to a more leisurely country back-road.

The Ridgeway stands aloof from the coming and going of

railways and motorways. Historians suggest that the Ridgeway is part of a much longer "green road" that stretched for some 250 miles across the width of England from the Wash in Norfolk down to the English Channel, probably somewhere near Lyme Regis. The fact that this pathway kept to the highest ground would seem to indicate that the lower ground, down on the plains and in the valleys, was difficult to cross because it was either densely wooded or marshy.

But it is entirely because the Ridgeway followed this highest possible path that it has continued to survive in its present, largely unspoilt, form. Throughout the length of the Ridgeway, from Streatley to West Kennett, you pass hardly any villages – a handful of farms but barely more than a few houses. This is because the Ridgeway runs above the spring line: without the ability to draw water there are no houses. Without houses and the construction of villages, the Ridgeway succeeded in avoiding the forces of change that affected life lower down in the valleys and on the plains.

But certain still-visible changes were wrought: the shaping of hill-tops into defensive forts and places of refuge during the uncertain times of the Iron Age.

Just to stand on the Ridgeway today is a unique experience; it is not too fanciful or pretentious to confess that you can feel its history. To cycle its entire length is a double achievement: you can claim not only that you have traversed one of Europe's oldest roads – but that you have enjoyed a great Mountain Bike Ride.

The history of the Ridgeway

The Ridgeway has become justifiably famous since the Countryside Commission opened its long-distance Ridgeway Path route in 1972. Largely following the line of the ancient Ridgeway drovers' road, this traverses what is recognised as great walking country; but walkers cannot realise its true potential.

The Ridgeway is famous, but only as a long-distance walkers' route linking the Thames at Streatley with Overton Hill, 40-odd miles away down near Avebury; the route ought to be even better known as the spine at the centre of a whole network of bridleways and byways which criss-cross the downs throughout its length.

They link villages to the north of the hills with others to the south, lowland racing stables with their upland gallops, farms with their distant fields. All routes whose designation is above that of a footpath are open to cyclists, which means mountain bikers have the run of the downs.

The Ridgeway itself is a green road and is open to all vehicles. The abundance of routes means it is easy to tailor a trip lasting anything from a couple of hours to a day, a weekend or a week. Walkers have to contend with the Ridgeway's remoteness. Very often you are five miles or more from the nearest source of drinking-water, let alone supplies of food or a bed for the night.

The village nestling in the valley which a walker must take half a day to reach can be coasted down to by the mountain biker in a matter of minutes.

There are many access points to the Ridgeway, and a handful of them are likely to be within relatively easy reach of anyone living in central southern England. What that means is that, given modern road communications, a unique stretch of wild and remote country, a southern wilderness, is on the doorstep of millions of cyclists.

This book identifies the access points, tells you what facilities you will find where, and outlines the routes which they open up to you. When the Countryside Commission laid out The Ridgeway Path they pushed on to the east of the Thames, following the line of another ancient route, the Icknield Way, another 40 miles to Ivinghoe Beacon near Tring. Stretches of that route are designated as a bridleway and can be cycled on. This stretch, however, is not on downland and does not provide the same network of paths that the Ridgeway does. For that reason, it is not covered in this book.

The hardwear and the softwear

The mountain bike

The cynic would say a mountain bike is an ordinary bike with a fancy paint job for those with more money than sense. Well, they are certainly more expensive and are no doubt seen as fashion accessories by some. However, a mountain bike has essential characteristics that set it apart.

It is designed for off-road use and is consequently more robust than the average touring bike. To cope with steep ascents it has 15, 18 or 21 gears and, to cope with fast and steep descents, much stronger brakes. Its tyres are designed to maximise traction rather than minimise rolling resistance, so they are fat and knobbly rather than narrow and smooth. To keep the weight down it dispenses with non-essentials such as mudguards.

History of the mountain bike

Mountain bikes were invented in Marin County, northern California, in the 1970s by a group with a penchant for bombing down dirt roads in forests and other remote places. No one was producing mountain bikes commercially at the time, and most machines were either hand-made to personal specifications or were heavily refined production models.

They used old-fashioned, hefty, large-tubed frames, often 20, 30 or 40 years old, but combined them with the then state-of-the-art 10-speed gearing of racing bikes. At first the bikes were only ridden downhill and transported back en masse in pick-up trucks. Then someone had the bright idea of riding uphill as well as down.

The first custom-built mountain bike frame was commissioned by Charles Kelly, which has earned him the title "Father of the Mountain Bike". Mountain bike frames were manufactured commercially in 1979. And the rest, as they say, is history.

Buying a bike: where to buy

You would not buy a car from a department store, nor should you purchase a bike from one. A mountain bike is going to take some rough treatment. You should buy from a specialist shop. You need to be able to take it back if it goes wrong and deal with someone who knows all about the machines. If the salesman also sells microwaves and dishwashers he is not likely to know much about the intricacies of your complex, delicate gearing system.

Most manufacturers do not assemble bikes completely. Final setting-up is left to the shop. You want to be sure that this was done by a bicycle mechanic, not someone who is more at home with hi-fis and videos.

Make sure the person selling to you knows his product. It is more likely in a small shop that the salesperson is the owner. Question them closely on the differences between bikes; don't let them blind you with science. If they rabbit on about STI etc. pin them down to what it means, how it works, why you need it.

Make it quite clear you want a bike for off-road use. Ask about after-sales service. A conscientious shopkeeper who wants you as a regular customer should offer a free service after a month or so. By then everything will have bedded in and adjustments will be needed.

Buying a bike: how much to spend

Mountain bikes do not differ greatly in essentials. Whatever surface distinction the exotic paint job may give, the machine beneath will probably have a frame and wheels made in Taiwan and a gearing and braking system from Japan.

The bike may have been designed in Europe or North America, but the vast majority will have been manufactured abroad. Sometimes a bike will bear the wording: "Hand built in England". Which is no doubt true, but can often mean simply that it arrived at the shop in bits and was hand built there.

Most manufacturers have a range of models, beginning with a basic bike at about £200, then going up in stages at roughly £300, £350, £400, £450, £650, £850 and on into the exotics at anything up to £2,000.

Decide how much you want to spend, then look for the bike that offers you the most for your money. The chances are you will find little to choose between competing models at a similar price. One of us narrowed our choice down to a Ridgeback and a Trek with a price difference of 20p. In terms of equipment they were identical. It was a toss-up which to buy.

Do not overlook details. One of us bought a bike with a foam-covered saddle. In wet weather it is not nice to sit on. The bike did not have a protective strip of metal or plastic to prevent the chain bouncing on it and chipping the paint. Small things, but important. If you find two bikes with little between them in engineering terms, look for the details which indicate how thoughtful the manufacturer has been in kitting the bike out.

Mountain bike anatomy

All these technical terms can seem like a foreign language to the layman, but they will help you communicate with the oily characters in the bike shop.

First the frame. It's a triangle, almost, with (moving anti-clockwise from the top) the top tube, the seat tube and the down tube. The tube up front that prevents the frame from quite becoming a triangle is the head tube, which links the front forks – which hold the wheel – and the handlebars.

Where seat tube and down tube meet is the bottom bracket, which holds the axle, to which the pedal cranks are attached. The two or three chain rings here make up the chainset. The thing which makes the chain switch between these chain rings is the front derailleur. The springy thing which dangles down beside the rear wheel and through which the chain threads is the rear derailleur, which shifts the chain from one rear sprocket to another. The controls on the handlebars with which you change gear are the thumb shifters.

Now, from the phrases above you should be able to stroll into a bike shop and make up impressive-sounding sentences such as "I have just gone bottom bracket over top tube, buckling my chainset and catching my thumb shifter in my rear derailleur. Please help."

Cycling off-road

Equipment

Some go for the lot, some for none. As with fell-walking, there are those who set off in a pair of old shoes and a tatty Parka, others who kit themselves out in full, fluorescent outfits, expensive footwear, helmets, gloves, backpacks, plastic map cases, the lot.

There is a vast industry dedicated to turning out high-fashion clothing and other accessories for mountain bikers. How much gear, and how high-fashion it is, is up to you. However, there are certain basic standards of equipment below which you are not safe off-road. Rough conditions require a certain amount of tough gear.

Fashionable, skin-tight cycle garb is not suitable for cycling in inclement conditions, because it does not conserve body heat. If you plan to cycle off-road for sustained periods, particularly in high country, you should ensure that you have clothes to keep you warm and dry in the worst conditions you might encounter. It is a good idea to wear several layers which you can peel off as you get hot and put on again as you cool off. Temperatures can drop dramatically when climbing – 3 degrees Fahrenheit per 1,000 ft is a fair average, which means that if you cycle up a 3,000-ft mountain the temperature is likely to drop 9 degrees Fahrenheit, more if weather conditions are adverse.

Footwear is a matter of taste. Trainers are light and comfortable, but if you are struggling over rough country you might prefer a light walking-boot.

The benefits of helmets are widely debated. Those in favour say they save lives, those against say that they encourage reckless behaviour because wearers feel safer when performing feats they would not consider without a helmet. All we can say is that, bouncing down a steep incline, ever conscious of the danger of being toppled over the handlebar by some rogue rock, we feel a lot safer in a helmet.

If you buy one, make sure that it conforms to British Safety Standards. It should be as close-fitting as possible and worn with the chin-strap tightly fastened. Once you have taken a tumble in a helmet, replace it, even if it does not seem damaged. Helmets work by absorbing the blow of an impact; they do not work well unless in pristine condition.

A basic tool kit is essential. One of us learnt that by being faced with a time-wasting five-mile walk because he did not have a puncture kit with him when cycling the Ridgeway. Neat little packs which strap on beneath the saddle or to the frame are ideal for carrying tools. You will need a puncture repair kit, spanners, screwdriver and Allen keys, plus a pump and a tool for removing and replacing links in the chain.

If you take the bike up fells or mountains you will have to carry it for periods. To stop the bike's hard, unyielding frame doing unspeakable damage to your soft one, pad the frame so that the bike can be shouldered comfortably. A shoulder sling which attaches inside the frame beneath the saddle is ideal.

Standing to the left of the bike, you can then slip your arm through the frame, balancing the bike with your right hand on the handlebars. These slings often incorporate a small triangular tool bag.

It can be a problem puzzling how to mount pump and water-bottle in such a way as not to impede carrying. Some people prefer to carry such things in a rucksack. Again, this is a question of personal taste.

One of the most important pieces of equipment you will need is a carrier for your car: there are dozens of designs available, from roof-rack types to those that attach to the boot or hatchback. We both have hatchbacks and find the latter the most suitable. They cost from around £35 and normally carry up to three bikes. Take care that these don't obscure your rear number plate, or you will be breaking the law.

Navigation
Ordnance Survey maps, where available the large-scale two and a half inch to the mile maps in the Outdoor Leisure series, are essential if you are to avoid getting lost or wasting time in taking wrong routes. This book has been designed for use in conjunction with a good map. On sustained off-road routes you should also take a compass. In poor visibility it will be invaluable. Getting lost can be extremely easy: much easier than you would ever have thought.

Fitness
Cycling is one of the best forms of exercise, but a long ride off-road will burn up a good deal of energy. Vigorous cycling, the sort you are likely to do plenty of on fells or downs, will burn up 7–10 calories a minute. Even after you have finished riding for the day, your metabolic rate remains high. You will feel warm for a couple of hours, and burn more calories because of it. You must eat well, otherwise you will burn up your energy stores and your performance will suffer.

Sensible, healthy eating is the key: plenty of high-fibre cereal, wholemeal bread, chicken, fish, raw vegetables, brown rice, pasta and fresh fruit. Take high-energy snacks with you, and an adequate supply of water. If your body fluid level drops by as little as two per cent greater heat loss results and performance suffers.

A mountain biker's code

The Sports Council and the Countryside Commission have drawn up a code of conduct for mountain bikers to which we heartily subscribe. Essential guidelines are:

Fasten all gates.
Leave no litter.
Do not harm wildlife, trees or plants.
Keep to rights of way across farmland.
Use gates and stiles to cross fences, hedges and walls.
Leave livestock, crops and machinery alone.
Guard against fire risks.
Help to keep all water clean.
Keep dogs under control.
Make no unnecessary noise.

In addition, if mountain biking is to improve its image it is important that all cyclists ride only where they are entitled to. Do not ride on public footpaths, where you have no legal right to be. Keep to bridleways, byways and green roads. On bridleways there is a public right to travel on horse or cycle. On bridleways, give way to walkers and horse-riders and remember that local authorities have the right to ban cyclists from bridleways if they wish. Do not be the one to give them an excuse to do so.

It also helps to be cheerful and polite. We make it a point to say "Hello" to everyone we meet on our travels (even if this merry greeting is met with the sort of look that suggests "Who is this cheerful lunatic on a pink bike . . . ?").

A naturalist's paradise . . .

Though it can seem a very natural environment, the chalk downlands are very much man-made. Forests once covered the chalklands, but because the soil was shallow the trees were easy to clear and the uplands were the first areas to be cultivated.

Before the advent of modern, chemically-aided farming, the poor soils could not be made to yield good crops and the land was used for grazing instead. The animals prevented the trees from returning and kept the grass short, creating an intricate texture of fine grasses, herbs and wild flowers – and a fine, springy turf.

The downs were once covered in such grassland but the advent of widespread arable farming on the uplands has reduced it enormously. Once-common plants which you might now only be sure of finding in nature reserves such as that at Seven Barrows near Lambourn include Thyme, Horseshoe Vetch, the Clustered Bellflower and Devil's-bit Scabious. Primroses and Cowslips are still common.

Butterflies which thrive in this environment include the Chalkhill Blue, the Small Skipper and the Marbled White. The downs are still rich in birdlife. Lapwings – black, white and dark green with a dab of orange under the tail and 12 inches (30 cm) from bill to tail – are common. Their "peewit" call is heard everywhere on the downs. Yellowhammers are also often seen, particularly on the hawthorn bushes and hedges at the fringe of the small, isolated copses. They are small, 6 inches (15 cm) from bill to tail. The male has a bright yellow head and breast, the female is darker. The warbling song of the skylark as it hovers high above its nest is also a common sound. Its back is streaked brown and it has white underparts and a streaked breast. Kestrels hunt small mammals over the open country. They are 15 inches (38 cm) long. Males are chestnut with black markings and a grey head and tail, females are darker.

You will see plenty of rabbits and perhaps a fox, weasel or stoat.

chapter 1

WEST KENNETT to BARBURY CASTLE

Introduction to the area

Finding the start of the Ridgeway is your first challenge. The map will tell you that the Long Distance Path begins at a spot on the A4 very near the village of West Kennett.

But no road sign offers any advance warning: no sign offers any information at all – not so much as a "This is the start (or end!) of the Ridgeway." The Ridgeway Cafe was the only landmark, but now even this has been razed. As you crest the brow of the hill, it's easy to flash past – brake too quickly and you could find yourself rear-ended by a milk lorry. Be prepared: approach slowly.

The first glimpse of the Ridgeway, at its junction with the A4 on Overton Hill, reveals nothing more than a shabby pull-in for cars and an unassuming track sloping its gentle way out of sight. If you come with great expectations of the Ridgeway, you could well be disappointed.

Your disappointment will not last long. On the 6-mile run up to Barbury Castle, you will see the best of the Ridgeway in all its moods. Wild open country, gentle tree-lined courses, mysterious tumuli, ancient stones, Iron Age forts – a great, wide, windswept scenery full of birdsong and wild flowers. In just 6 miles, your crash-course introduction to the Ridgeway will leave you hooked – craving more of its raw scenic beauty.

You will also discover some of the Ridgeway's less pleasant surprises: a path so heavily rutted in places that in bad weather you will find almost impassable bogs – cloying mud that grabs your wheels in an iron grip. In dry weather, the hard ruts can snatch at your pedals and threaten to toss you head-first into a ditch.

Apart from glorious views – at first a magnificent sweep of countryside over Windmill Hill and the North Wiltshire Downs, later the less stirring sight of the city of Swindon glimpsed across wide, open fields – there are no major sights or villages on this stretch of the Ridgeway.

The route

The first 6 miles (9.6 km) of the Ridgeway.

Mostly gentle ascent through 104 yds over 5 miles (95 m over 8 km) from Overton Hill to Uffcott Down.
Slight descent of 42 yds over 1 mile (38 m over 1.6 km) from Uffcott Down to Barbury Castle.
Nearly all of the journey is on a rough, stony path – sometimes heavily rutted.

The Ridgeway officially begins at a small pull-in for cars, a quarter of a mile east of West Kennett on the A4: there is nearly always room to park here. The path runs directly north: it climbs fairly sharply over the first ½-mile (0.8 km), and then levels off for a mostly flat ride to Barbury Castle.

For almost the whole length of this stretch, the Ridgeway is stony and in several parts quite deeply rutted. In the places with the deepest ruts, proceed slowly and choose a route carefully. If you go into a rut, your pedals clip the sides and it's easy to tip over – if you're going fairly quickly, this can be dangerous.

After almost 2 miles, the Ridgeway has its first junction – a "green street" coming up from the left, leading down to the village of Avebury. After a further 2 miles, the Ridgeway crosses the B4041 road which runs down Fiddler's Hill towards Broad Hinton.

Shortly before Barbury Castle – where the path deviates from the "true" historic course of the Ridgeway – the official long-distance trail crosses a partly metalled road which runs down to the centre of Wroughton. At the eastern side of the Castle, from the Barbury Castle Country Park, another road goes down to Wroughton past the military hospital.

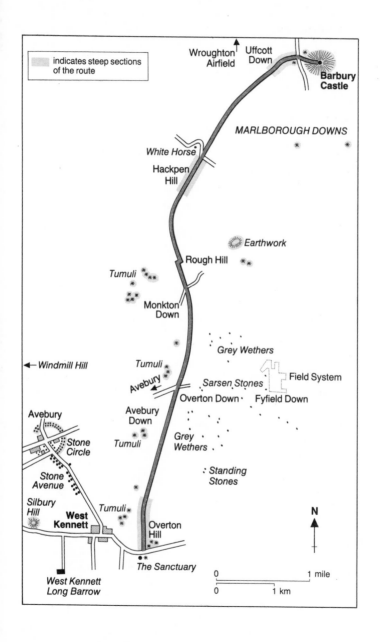

indicates steep sections
of the route

Wroughton
Airfield

Uffcott
Down

**Barbury
Castle**

MARLBOROUGH DOWNS

White Horse

Hackpen
Hill

Earthwork

Rough Hill

Tumuli

Monkton
Down

Grey Wethers

Tumuli

Field System

Avebury

Sarsen Stones

← *Windmill Hill*

Overton Down

Fyfield Down

Avebury
Down

Avebury

*Grey
Wethers*

*Stone
Circle*

Tumuli

*Stone
Avenue*

∴ *Standing
Stones*

*Silbury
Hill*

N

**West
Kennett**

Tumuli

Overton
Hill

The Sanctuary

*West Kennett
Long Barrow*

0   1 mile

0   1 km

Along the whole of this stretch, the Ridgeway is clearly marked and easy to follow: take care, shortly before Barbury Castle, that you take the Ridgeway National Trail, rather than the old course of the Ridgeway, also marked, which pursues a quite different route.

What you will see

Before you begin your journey on the Ridgeway, you will want to spare time to take in some of the many ancient sites that are all within a short bike ride of Overton Hill. (In fact, you may decide that it makes sense to begin your Ridgeway ride from the village of Avebury, which has good car parking, a pub, restaurant and other facilities, as well as a direct link to the Ridgeway: see "Other routes" below.)

About a mile and a half from the official start of the Ridgeway at Overton Hill lies the village of Avebury with its extraordinary Late Neolithic circle of sarsens or standing stones which almost completely encircle the village. As with Stonehenge, its closely related neighbour to the south which was built in 1500 BC at roughly the same time as Avebury, no one is entirely sure what purpose the stone circle served.

In a lot of ways, Avebury is a far greater achievement than Stonehenge – in the seventeenth century, antiquarian John Aubrey said Avebury surpassed Stonehenge "as a cathedral does a parish church". Standing on the circle, with a clear blue sky vaulted over your head like a cathedral dome, it's difficult not to be stirred by the art of those ancient builders.

About 100 huge stones, many weighing over 40 tons, together with a large bank and ditch, enclose an area of more than 28 acres. If you want to find out more about Avebury and its history, the Alexander Keiller Museum, housed in what was the coach house of Avebury Manor, has a good collection of finds and explanatory displays.

About 1½ miles (2.4 km) south of Avebury is West Kennett Long Barrow, reached by footpath from the A4. This is a large tomb that dates from 2500 BC and was in continuous use for almost a thousand years – it may have been something like the mausoleum of a ruling family of the period.

Lying immediately next to the A4, almost midway between West Kennett Long Barrow and Avebury, is Silbury Hill – which seems to have served no obvious purpose. This is an entirely man-made hill, 130 feet high (40 m) and covering 5½ acres. The effort involved in building the hill must have been extraordinary, as the workers would have had nothing more than antler-picks, crude shovels made from the shoulder blades of oxen and pieces of wood with which to move the earth.

The Sanctuary, the final site worth a visit, lies immediately across the A4 from the start of the Ridgeway. If you can, approach the Sanctuary from Avebury village by coming down the road that follows the processional way called the Avenue. There is now little to see at the site of the Sanctuary – another structure whose purpose defies investigation by archaeologists.

Further south of the site of the Sanctuary beyond the village of East Kennett, about 1 mile (1.6 km) from Overton Hill – along the line of the old Ridgeway – are well-preserved remains of the Wansdyke. The Wansdyke was a defensive ditch, built some time after the Romans, which ran from Inkpen to the Bristol Channel near Portishead. Who built it, and why they wanted to defend themselves, hasn't been fully explained.

Across the A4 from the Sanctuary, at the start of the Ridgeway, on your left as you look up the path, used to stand the Ridgeway Cafe. A bizarre plan to build an "Iron Age" hotel here failed to gain the approval of the planners. The site was acquired by the National Trust, which has returned the area to grassland.

Moving up the Ridgeway path, you pass through something of a Megalithic theme park: on both sides are important archaeological sites: various barrows, sarsen stones ("grey wethers", as they are called), tumuli and assorted mounds. About 2 miles (3.2 km) from Overton Hill, at the junction of the path of Avebury, to the right is the entrance to the Fyfield Downs Nature Reserve.

These downs are one of the largest remaining tracts of high chalk downland in England containing natural deposits of sarsen stones. The area also has some of the best-preserved Celtic and medieval field systems in Britain. Five minutes from the Ridgeway is the field where you can see a "river" of the huge stones – hundreds of megalithic building bricks ready to construct another Stonehenge or Avebury.

Nearly 4 miles (6.4 km) from Overton Hill, above Berwick Bassett Down, can be seen the Neolithic camp of Windmill Hill, beyond the village of Winterbourne Monkton.

The airfield visible from a long stretch of the Ridgeway is Wroughton, a Second World War base which is now owned by the London Science Museum and houses its collection of aircraft. The Museum holds a series of open days at Wroughton in order to display the collection.

Famous connections

In the village of Avebury lives the writer and broadcaster Ludovic Kennedy, who has played a leading role in the "Avebury in Danger" campaign to prevent unsympathetic tourist development. Other campaigners include former government minister Lord Kennett, who also lives in the village.

The man who perhaps did most to preserve Avebury was Alexander Keiller, whose family fortunes derived from Keiller marmalade. Keiller, who was the last private owner of Avebury, was an enthusiastic member of the Society of Antiquaries and paid for extensive archaeological work in the village.

In 1942, the site was bought by the National Trust – the Manor, however, remained in private hands. The Manor has been at the centre of a bitter controversy following its acquisition by a St Albans builder who developed it as an "Elizabethan Experience".

Other routes in the area

Circuit from Avebury via the Ridgeway Path and West Kennett: 5 miles (8 km).

Ascent of 73 yds over 1½ miles (67 m over 2.4 km) from the centre of Avebury to the Ridgeway.

Descent of 57 yds over 2 miles (53 m over 3.2 km) to the A4 at Overton Hill.

One and a half miles (2.4 km) on metalled road from Overton Hill back to Avebury.

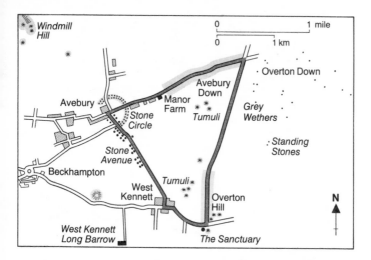

From the centre of the village cross the B4003 road, up past the
Red Lion pub, heading roughly north-east down a metalled lane.
After about ½ a mile (0.8 km), near the entrance to Manor
Farm, the lane becomes a rough track and starts a steep ascent
towards the Ridgeway.

After 1 mile (1.6 km), you reach the Ridgeway, where you turn
right for a fast downwards run towards Overton Hill and the A4
(take care of the ruts and loose stones). At the A4 turn right
towards West Kennett village. Half-way through the village,
near the entrance to West Kennett Farm, turn right up the
"Stone Avenue" towards Avebury and your original starting-
point.

**Circuit from Manton Down to Fyfield Down returning via the
Ridgeway and A4: 8¾ miles (14 km).**
Slight ascent from car park at Manton Down to Fyfield Down,
37 yards over 1½ miles (34 m over 2.4 km).
Small dip from Fyfield Down to Ridgeway: 1 mile (1.6 km).
Descent down the Ridgeway to Overton Hill, 55 yards over 1¾
miles (51 m over 2.8 km).
Mostly level ride from Overton Hill down the A4 to Manton: 3½
miles (5.6 km).

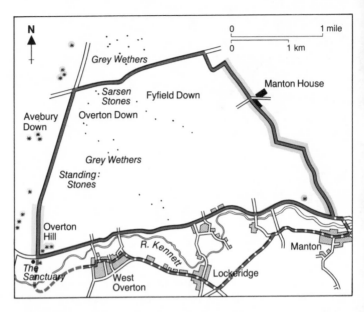

Climb from Manton to Manton Down, 66 yards over 1¾ miles (61 m over 2.8 km).
Five and a quarter miles over metalled road.

In Manton village follow signs for Manton House. Follow the road up the hill until you reach the "Private Road" sign at the entrance to Manton House where you will find a large public car park (watch out for the racehorses on the road on the way to the gallops).

From the car park follow the signs to "Avebury" and cycle up the well-made road to the reservoir at the top of the hill. Turn left and follow the track to Fyfield and Overton Downs. Continue along the bridleway, and through the gates, until you reach the Ridgeway. At Overton Hill on the A4, turn left to Marlborough. At Manton, turn left up to Manton House and return to the car park.

As an alternative to the fast way back along the A4, you could make a longer diversion by heading across the A4 at Overton Hill and returning to Manton via West Overton and Lockeridge.

Facilities

AVEBURY

A small village with the basic amenities of a pub, post office and general stores.

Pubs

Red Lion Inn, High Street, Avebury (067 23 266).
Stones Restaurant, Great Barn, Avebury (067 23 514).

SWINDON

The biggest town in the vicinity of the Ridgeway (the start at Overton Hill is 15 miles from the town centre). Swindon is an old railway town which is now rather charmless. It has a good range of hotels and a fast train service to London (55 minutes to Paddington) – so it makes a good base. British Rail passenger information: 0793 536804.

Hotels

Holiday Inn, Pipers Way, Swindon SN3 1SH (0793 512121).
Post House, Marlborough Road, Swindon SN3 6AQ (0793 24601).
Crest, Oxford Road, Swindon SN3 4TL (0793 831333).

Cycle shops

The Cycling Centre, 233 Ferndale Road, Swindon (0793 536657).
Express Cycle Specialists, 96–99 Manchester Road, Swindon (0793 534907).
Cycle Discount Store, 27 Shrivenham Road, Swindon (0793 523306).

WROUGHTON

Wroughton Airfield (0793 814466): home of the Science Museum's transport collection, claimed to be the UK's biggest. There are over 1,000 exhibits, which are displayed during open days, one day a month, through the summer.

Tourist information

Avebury: The Great Barn, Avebury, Wiltshire SN8 1RF (067 23 425).
Swindon: 32 The Arcade, Brunel Centre, Swindon, Wiltshire SN1 1LN (0793 530328).

chapter 2

BARBURY CASTLE to FOX HILL

Introduction to the area

There is no castle with drawbridge, moat, turrets or damsels in distress at Barbury: this "castle" is actually an Iron Age fort that was in use until Saxon times. According to the Anglo-Saxon Chronicle, the invading Saxon forces scored a victory over the Roman-British on the lower slopes of Barbury Hill.

Nowadays it has been turned into a "Country Park" (becoming a country park seems to involve little more than building a car park, public toilets and opening an information office). On warm, sunny Sundays, this is a popular spot for picnickers.

But on your bike, you can leave the crowds behind in a couple of minutes. The 10-mile (16-km) ride to Fox Hill is something of a switchback journey through glorious, rapidly changing countryside. The first part of the journey is across open downland; as you approach Ogbourne St George, the countryside becomes lusher and more gentle. Ogbourne St George, skirted by the Ridgeway, is one of those fantastically picturesque villages, with thatched cottages and a babbling brook, that one imagines exist only on chocolate boxes.

After the climb from Ogbourne St George to Round Hill Downs and towards Liddington, the scenery changes again. On one ride up from Ogbourne, near Round Hill Downs, a fox ambled out of the hedgerow and padded on ahead with its lithe, rolling gait, hardly bothering to look around.

Large fields of crops, give way once more to the wild, wuthering heights of Liddington. The top of Liddington Hill, another Iron Age fort, boasts a stubby clump of windswept beech trees, a familiar landmark to any regular travellers on the M4.

The ride down from Liddington to Fox Hill takes you across

the M4, and the countryside changes once more to softer, tree-lined roads and more sheltered cycling.

The route

Ten miles (16 km) from Barbury Castle to Fox Hill.

Mostly gentle descent through 120 yds over 3½ miles (112 m over 5.6 km) from Barbury Castle to Ogbourne St George.
From Ogbourne St George to Round Hill Downs, steep climb of 98 yds over 1 mile (92 m over 1.6 km).
Mostly flat ride from Round Hill Downs to Liddington Hill, climb of 6½ yds over 2½ miles (6 m over 4 km).
From Liddington Hill to Fox Hill, rapid descent of 89 yards over 3 miles (83 m over 4.8 km).
The last mile of the ride from the bottom of Liddington Hill is on metalled road.
Most of the journey is on a rough, stony path – sometimes heavily rutted; in bad weather, long stretches can be extremely muddy.

Barbury Castle with a large car park and easy access from Junction 15 of the M4, 5 miles (8 km) away via Chiseldon – and 5½ miles (9 km) from Swindon railway station – makes an excellent base for exploring the Ridgeway, either west to Avebury or east to Uffington and the White Horse.

As you leave the car park at Barbury Castle, heading south-east towards Ogbourne St George, you need to be extremely careful not to take the wrong route. The obvious track in front of you will take you south to Marlborough. Unfortunately, at the time of writing, the Ridgeway Path sign which will send you in the right direction had disappeared – look out for the turning to the left shortly after Upper Herdswick Farm: an inconspicuous "Ridgeway Path" is attached to the gate that guards the path. This path will take you along Smeathe's Ridge.

On the descent towards Ogbourne St George, the number of gates over which you will have to lug your bike will give you plenty of opportunity to stop and enjoy the views north and south. Near Ogbourne, you turn right on to the metalled road for a couple of hundred yards before the Ridgeway signs divert you around the village.

After swinging left across the A345 Marlborough to Swindon

road at Southend, and after passing through the arch of a bridge that once carried a railway south from Swindon to Hampshire, the path begins to climb sharply.

At Rodden Hill Downs, after crossing the Ogbourne to Aldbourne road, the path continues flat and mostly straight towards Liddington Hill before dropping down to Fox Hill.

As on the first stretch, you need to take great care in the places that are rutted or muddy.

What you will see

If there aren't too many visitors about, Barbury Castle is a great place to sit and enjoy the views. Barbury is the first of a series of hill forts you will encounter on the Ridgeway: further on there are Liddington, Uffington and Segsbury. They are called "Iron Age"; however, archaeologists find it difficult to be sure about the precise date of their construction.

The best estimate is that like other hill forts of its type Barbury dates back to around 500 BC – although some archaeologists

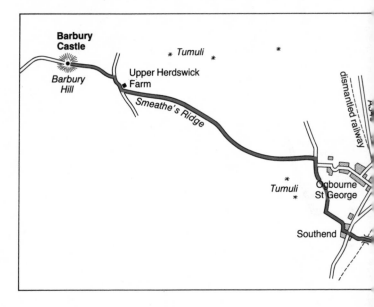

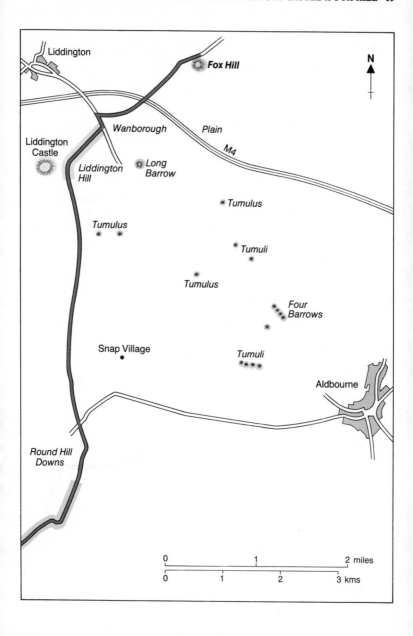

argue that the Ridgeway forts could be far older.

Barbury is one of the best examples of a hill fort, dominating the countryside to the north and south – as well as guarding the line of the Ridgeway itself, the prime artery of communication.

It's worth making a small detour off the Ridgeway to visit Ogbourne St George, a village situated at one of the highest points of the Marlborough downs. This is an English village as sweet as anything you can find in the Cotswolds. The end of the village nearest to the main road promises nothing special, but further investigation offers greater riches – including a lovely church and a fine manor house built on the site of an eleventh-century priory. Now by-passed by the mainroad, Ogbourne St George maintains a delightfully unhurried existence.

As you begin the climb from Ogbourne St George you will pass through an old railway bridge of the Midland and South Western Junction Railway. The line was built in 1881 to offer a through route from the Midlands to the South Coast, and to provide a much-needed service from Swindon to Marlborough and Andover, with stations at Chiseldon and Ogbourne. It proved to be commercially successful through most of its life – in the preparations for D-Day in 1944 the line was in use 24 hours a day. However, passenger services were withdrawn in 1961. Happily a lot of work has been done to convert the disused line into a cycleway.

A detour worth making after the climb from Ogbourne St George is to seek out the "ghost village" of Snap (see "Other routes" below). Snap was a village deliberately abandoned to provide grazing land for sheep. In *The Oldest Road: the Ridgeway* J.R.L. Anderson writes:

The Highland Clearances in Scotland are described in all the history books: the dispossession of a few inarticulate peasants in Wiltshire was not on a sufficient scale to pull the national heartstrings. Yet it is sad that sheep should be deemed more profitable than men and women. Snap is an archaeological site now – the church, the foundations of cottages, the alignment of the village street, nice subjects for a doctoral thesis.

If you climb to the top of Liddington Hill, you will have reached the highest point of the downs at 277 metres (303 yards).

Famous connections

The two people most closely associated with this stretch of the Ridgeway are Richard Jefferies and his biographer, the poet and writer Edward Thomas.

Richard Jefferies was born in the village of Coate, now a suburb of Swindon, in 1848; his home there is now the Richard Jefferies Museum. Jefferies was one of the first writers and commentators on affairs of the countryside – a pioneer of the newspaper "country diary". He was a highly prolific writer, who until his death from tuberculosis at the age of 39 wrote nine novels and hundreds of newspaper and magazine articles.

In his "spiritual autobiography", *The Story of My Heart*, Jefferies wrote of how as a young man he would climb Liddington Hill "to breathe a new air and to have a fresher aspiration":

Moving up the sweet, short turf, at every step my heart seemed to obtain a wider horizon of feeling: with every inhalation of rich, pure air a deeper desire. The very light of the sun was whiter and more brilliant here. By the time I had reached the summit I had entirely forgotten the petty circumstances and the annoyances of existence. I felt myself, myself. There was an intrenchment on the summit, and going down into the fosse, I walked round it slowly to recover breath. On the south-western side there was a spot where the outer bank had partially slipped, leaving a gap. There the view was over a broad plain, beautiful with wheat and inclosed by a perfect amphitheatre of green hills. Through these hills there was one narrow groove, or pass, southwards where the white clouds seemed to close in the horizon. Woods hid the scattered hamlets and farmhouses, so that I was quite alone. I was utterly alone with the sun and earth. Lying down on the grass, I spoke in my soul to the earth, the sun, the air and the distant sea far beyond sight.

It is fitting that Jefferies has a memorial at the top of Liddington Hill, looking out over the place he wrote about with such affection.

Edward Thomas was born in London in 1878, the son of a railway clerk. Like Jefferies, in order to earn enough to live, Thomas had to maintain a prolific output as a writer and poet.

As a poet, he is best remembered for "Adlestrop", a poem about the name of a Cotswold village, written not long before his death in 1917 fighting in France in the First World War:

Yes, I remember Adlestrop –
The name, because one afternoon
Of heat the express-train drew up there
Unwontedly. It was late June.

Thomas shared Jefferies' passion for the countryside, and he visited the places on and around the Ridgeway that had influenced Jefferies. In 1909 Thomas wrote *The Life of Richard Jefferies*, revisiting the Ridgeway:

Best of all the Down Ways is the Ridgeway . . . Jefferies knew it well; this above all others would take him past "hill after hill and plain after plain" in silence and solitude. It passes under Liddington Hill, with little risings and fallings through the open corn-land, but, climbing almost to Barbury Castle, it keeps a great height along the top of Hackpen Hill, paving itself with harebell, silverweed, eyebright and bartsia; now east, now west, now south, it commands vast soaring and diving grounds for the delighted eyes, among solitary slopes of green and white hills, of turf and cloud.

Other routes in the area

Circuit from Barbury Castle to Ogbourne St Andrew returning via the Ridgeway Path: 8½ miles (13.6 km).
Descent of 125 yds over 4 miles (75 m over 6.4 km) from Barbury Castle to Ogbourne St Andrew.
Level ride of 1½ miles (2.4 km) from Ogbourne St Andrew to Ogbourne St George.
Ascent of 125 yds over 3 miles (75 m over 4.8 km) from Ogbourne St George back to Barbury Castle.

Leave the car park at Barbury Castle as if you were following the Ridgeway towards Ogbourne St George – but instead of turning left after Upper Herdswick Farm for Smeathe's Ridge, continue straight down the path in front of you, adjacent to the gallops.

On reaching the road at the bottom of the hill near the sign

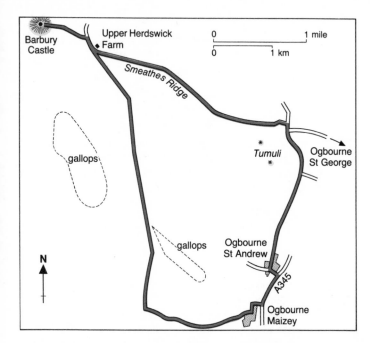

"By-way to Barbury Castle" turn left to Ogbourne Maizey. Pass through the village, turn left at A345; after 500 yds (450 m) turn left at the war memorial into Ogbourne St Andrew. Go through the village; before the last house – a bungalow – on the left, take the track towards Ogbourne St George.

Follow the Ridgeway Path (above), in reverse, back to Barbury Castle.

Circuit from Ogbourne St George to Snap village, returning via the Ridgeway Path: 7 miles (11.2 km).
Steep climb of 103 yards over 1 mile (95 m over 1.6 km) from Ogbourne St George to Round Hill Downs.
Level ride of 1¼ miles (2 km) from Round Hill Downs to turn-off for Upper Upham.
Small dip to Upham, steeper descent and climb from Upham to Woodsend: fall and climb of 60 yards over ¾ of a mile (55 m over 1.2 km).

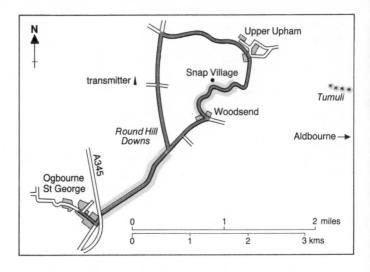

Level ride for 2 miles (3.2 km) on road from Woodsend to downhill turn-off for Ridgeway.
Descent of 72 yards over ¾ of a mile (66 m over 1.2 km) from downhill turn-off to A345 Marlborough to Swindon road.
Level ½ mile (0.8 km) ride back to Ogbourne St George. Three miles (4.8 km) of the ride are on metalled road.

Park in the centre of the village, cycle out under the elevated A345 on the metalled Copse Drove towards Aldbourne. The climb towards the top of the hill is hard work – if you get off and push, you can at least enjoy the views to the west.

At the top of the hill, pick up the Ridgeway to your left, travelling north. Continue across one junction which to your left leads to a large transmitter. At the next junction take the right turn to Upper Upham (continue straight on leaving the Ridgeway, continuing to your left). A quick drop and ascent takes you to Upham Farm: go straight through the farm until you reach a sign "By-way", next to a red pillar box, which directs you down a delightful tree-lined road.

This road is the start of a precipitous helter-skelter descent, and then a steep climb towards Woodsend – with the site of Snap village (see above) to your right. When you reach the metalled road turn right towards Ogbourne St George until, after a mile, "Ridgeway Path" is signposted to the left. Follow the Ridgeway back down to the A345. Turn right, then after 150 yards (137 m) turn left towards Ogbourne St George.

Facilities

BARBURY CASTLE

There is a large car park, and toilets. On summer Sundays, you may also find an ice-cream van.

MARLBOROUGH

Marlborough is an attractive market town, which has been in existence in one form or another since Roman times – and officially a "borough" since 1204. It is perhaps best known today for Marlborough College, which stands at the west end of the town – one of the most expensive private schools in Britain. It has a good range of shops, pubs and restaurants.

Accommodation

Ivy House, High Street, Marlborough SN8 1HJ (0672 515333).
Castle and Ball, High Street, Marlborough SN8 1LZ (0672 55201).

Pubs

Green Dragon, 12 High Street, Marlborough (0672 52366).
Lamb Hotel, The Parade, Marlborough (0672 52668).
Roebuck Inn, London Road, Marlborough (0672 52610).

Cycle shop

Town Mill Cycles, Angel Yard, Marlborough (0672 54914).

OGBOURNE ST GEORGE

A small, very attractive village with a shop and two pubs.

Pubs

The Old Crown, Ogbourne St George (067 284 445).
Parklands Hotel (067 284 000).

Tourist information

Marlborough: St Peter's Church, High Street, Marlborough, Wiltshire SN8 1HQ (0672 53989).

chapter 3

FOX HILL to THE WHITE HORSE

Introduction to the area

Displaying what seems to be an almost infinite capacity to transform itself, on this section the Ridgeway adopts yet another new guise, this time taking on a rather more mellow shape. It can certainly be wild and windswept – when you reach the top of Uffington Castle prepare to be blown off your feet.

However, the gentle sweep of downs and the exquisite views north and south provide a memorable 5½ mile (8.8 km) ride.

If it weren't for the fearsome ruts and – in wet weather – large, swampy patches of mud, this stretch would be one of the best to cycle. (It's pleasing to report, however, that much-needed restoration work to the Ridgeway is in hand on the stretch between Wayland's Smithy and Uffington Castle.)

After a brisk climb up from Fox Hill, the Ridgeway levels off before its final assault on Uffington Castle and the White Horse. Here, on the mid-way part of the Ridgeway, is one of the most solitary stretches. Apart from visitors around Uffington Castle and Wayland's Smithy, you are unlikely to encounter many other people.

The route

Five and a half miles (8.8 km) from Fox Hill to Uffington Castle.

The early part of the ride involves a fairly steep climb through 59 yds over ½ a mile (54 m over 0.8 km) from Fox Hill to the southern shoulder of Charlbury Hill.

From Charlbury Hill to Ridgeway Farm there is a brisk descent of 56 yds over 1 mile (51 m over 1.6 km).

Mostly flat ride for 2½ miles (4 km) from Ridgeway Farm to Wayland's Smithy.

From Wayland's Smithy to Uffington Castle: climb of 59 yards over 1½ miles (54 m over 2.4 km).

From Liddington Hill to Fox Hill, rapid descent of 89 yards over 3 miles (83 m over 4.8 km).

Apart from 200 yds at the start, the whole of the journey is on rough track – some of it very rough.

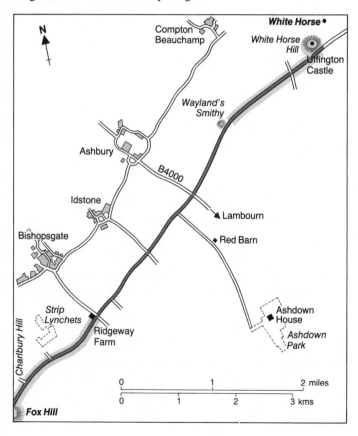

After a brief road section which began at the foot of Liddington Hill and continues across the M4, the Ridgeway proper begins again 200 yds after The Shepherd's Rest, where it branches off to the right. The route is well signposted throughout.

There is a large car park (for patrons) at The Shepherd's Rest, and another at the re-start of the Ridgeway 200 yds further on. Four miles (6.4 km) from the centre of Swindon and a 10-minute drive from Junction 15 of the M4, Fox Hill is a good base for exploring the Ridgeway.

After an early climb and then rapid descent to Ridgeway Farm, the Ridgeway continues flat and straight to Wayland's Smithy. The path at this point is easily accessible from a series of villages that lie at the foot of the downs on a road which shadows the Ridgeway. Bishopstone, Idstone, Ashbury and Compton Beauchamp all lie within 1½ miles (2.4 km) of each other – and within ½ a mile of the Ridgeway.

In many places, the Ridgeway is very rutted – and depending on the weather, mud can make it difficult going.

Shortly before Wayland's Smithy, you cross the B4000 road from Lambourn to Ashbury.

What you will see

The first part of the ride, beyond Ridgeway Farm, offers breathtaking views but little in the way of genuine sights. Shortly before Ridgeway Farm, the Ordnance Survey map marks the site of "Strip lynchets" to the left of the Ridgeway. Lynchets are ancient terraced fields, a typical feature of the White Horse Downs; like the terraces of vines in the Mediterranean, these lynchets were probably built up to create an area to grow crops.

Ridgeway Farm is eerily deserted, scraps of plastic flapping against fences, doors banging in the wind on squeaky hinges – alone in such a solitary spot, it's easy to imagine this is how life might be after Armageddon.

One and a half miles after Ridgeway Farm, a turning to the right towards the Red Barn allows access to Ashdown House, a house built in chalk in the Dutch style by the first Earl of Craven in around 1665 for Charles I's sister Elizabeth, the Queen of Bohemia.

Ashdown House was described by Sir Nikolaus Pevsner as "the perfect doll's house", and this is indeed how it looks – albeit a very Dutch-looking doll's house.

The main feature of the house, now owned by the National Trust, is a great staircase that climbs from hall to attic – there is access to the roof, which offers splendid views. There are also handsome grounds and a deer park.

One and a quarter miles after the turn-off to Ashdown House is one of the Ridgeway's most famous sites: Wayland's Smithy. It stands in a little copse of trees a short walk off the Ridgeway. According to legend, if you left your horse here, with a coin on the lintel stone, you would return the following morning to find that it had been shod by Wayland, the blacksmith of the Saxon gods.

Wayland's Smithy is actually a Megalithic long barrow – a Neolithic burial chamber that dates back to almost 3000 BC, long before the Saxons and their gods came to England.

The section of the Ridgeway from Wayland's Smithy to Uffington Castle on White Horse Hill is perhaps the most photographed section of the entire Long Distance Path. The great bulk of White Horse Hill, when first glimpsed, is truly impressive. The climb up the hill is however rather steep: 47 yards over 1 mile (43 m over 1.6 m).

To reach Uffington Castle you will need to leave the Ridgeway at the top of White Horse Hill, climb over a stile and scramble up the "castle's" grassy ramparts. Even on a relatively calm day, a brisk wind blows which can make the climb even more difficult – but the effort is worth it.

The springy grass is sprinkled with an extraordinary variety of wild flowers, particularly orchids. The point to make for is, of course, the White Horse. Standing above the Horse, you cannot enjoy its subtle design (you need to be up above in an aeroplane or standing about 2 miles away, down in the Vale, to appreciate fully its composition – sitting in a British Rail high-speed train travelling between Swindon and Paddington offers one of the best views!).

There are many white horses in England, but there are reasons to suppose that this was one of the first. It used to be believed that the horse was cut into the turf to commemorate Alfred's victory over the Danes at the Battle of Ashdown in AD 871. Archaeological evidence, however, suggests that the horse goes back to a much earlier date, possibly the first century BC.

When seen at a distance, the design seems thoroughly modern, something that a bank or oil company would want to use as a logo. It's extraordinary that someone 2,000 years ago, working on such a large scale, could capture the grace and easy movement of a horse in full stride.

English Heritage is nowadays charged with the job of keeping the outlines of the horse clear and white (some job: the beast is 120 yds long by 53 yds high: 110 m by 49 m). Until the last century, however, the "scouring" of the White Horse was a good excuse for local fun and games. (Thomas Hughes describes the revelries in *The Scouring of the White Horse*: see below.)

White Horse Hill is rich in legends. On the west side of the hill is a hollow known as The Manger (because, of course, this is where the White Horse came down to eat). The stumpy, flat-topped mound in front of the White Horse is known as Dragon Hill: upon it St George is said to have fought and killed the dragon (legend has it that the grassless patches on the hill are where the dragon's blood flowed).

Famous connections

Thomas Hughes, the author of *Tom Brown's Schooldays*, was born in Uffington in 1822. Like Tom Brown, Thomas Hughes went to Rugby School and then to Oriel College, Oxford, before becoming a barrister, a Liberal MP and eventually a county court judge at Chester. He died in 1896 at the age of 73.

Although he wrote other things, *Tom Brown's Schooldays* is the work for which Hughes is best remembered. The opening of the novel concentrates on Uffington and the White Horse Hill. Uffington School, attended in the novel by Tom Brown, is now Tom Brown's School Museum.

And then what a hill is the White Horse Hill! There it stands right up above all the rest, nine hundred feet above the sea, and the boldest, bravest shape for a chalk hill that you ever saw. Let us go up to the top of him, and see what is to be found there . . . Here, right up on

the highest point, from which they say you can see eleven counties . . .
The ground falls away rapidly on all sides. Was there ever such turf
in the whole world? You sink up to your ankles at every step, and yet
the spring of it is delicious . . . It is altogether a place that you won't
forget – a place to open a man's soul and make him prophesy, as he
looks down on that great Vale, spread out as the garden of the Lord
before him, and wave on wave of the mysterious downs behind; and
to the right and left the chalk hills running away into the distance . . .

John Betjeman and his wife Penelope lived in 1934 at Garrards
Farm in Uffington. He later recalled his life there in a poem:

> *. . . those spontaneous Berkshire days*
> *In straw-thatched chalk-built pre-War Uffington*
> *Before the March of Progress had begun*
> *When all the world seemed waiting to be won*
> *When evening air with mignonette was scented*
> *And picture windows had not been invented*
> *When shooting foxes still was thought unsporting*
> *And White Horse Hill was still the place for courting.*

Other routes in the area

Circuit from Fox Hill via the Ridgeway to Idstone, returning
on metalled road through Bishopstone: 8 miles (12.8 km).
The early part of the ride involves a fairly steep climb through
59 yds over ½ a mile (54 m over 0.8 km) from Fox Hill to the
southern shoulder of Charlbury Hill.
From Charlbury Hill to Ridgeway Farm there is a brisk descent
of 56 yds over 1 mile (51 m over 1.6 km).
Mostly flat ride for 1¾ miles (2.8 km) from Ridgeway Farm to
Ashbury turn-off.
Steep descent from Ridgeway path down to Ashbury, 73 yds over
½ a mile (67 m over 0.8 km).
Level ride to Bishopstone for 1¾ miles (2.8 km).
Steep climb and descent for return to Fox Hill, 60 yds over 2
miles (55 m over 3.2 km).
Four and three-quarter miles (7.6 km) on metalled road.

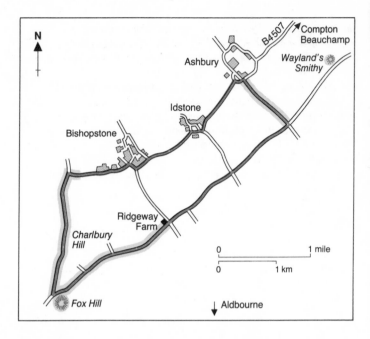

Because the road from Bishopstone to Ashbury – which then becomes the B4507 – so closely shadows the Ridgeway, this is a circular tour you can extend or shorten according to taste. On this tour, you turn off towards Ashbury; if you wish, you could turn off earlier at Bishopstone or Idstone – or just as simply carry on to Compton Beauchamp, or even as far as Kingston Lisle.

Although the return half of the journey is on road, there is little traffic to worry about. Using the road also means that you have the pleasure of passing through a selection of delightful villages – particularly Bishopstone.

To start the tour, follow the Ridgeway path as detailed above. About 1¾ miles (2.8 km) after passing Ridgeway Farm, turn left for the fast 1-in-10 ride down to Ashbury. Turn left at Ashbury post office and follow the road towards Bishopstone. After Bishopstone, follow the signs for Aldbourne and Marlborough: there's a hard climb up Charlbury Hill before a gentle descent back to your starting-point.

Circuit from the Ridgeway car park at Ashbury Hill to Ashdown Park and Wayland's Smithy: 6¼ miles (10 km).

Ashbury Hill to Idstone junction, via the Ridgeway: ¾ of a mile (1.2 km).

Idstone junction to Ashdown Park road junction at B4000: a descent of 48 yards over 2 miles (44 m over 3.2 km).

Ashdown Park road junction at B4000 to Tower Hill: climb of 75 yards over 1 mile (69 m over 1.6 km) on metalled road.

From Tower Hill to Knighton junction on the Ridgeway: mostly level ride of 1½ miles (2.4 km).

From Knighton junction to Ashbury hill car park: mostly level ride of 1 mile (1.6 km).

One mile on metalled road.

Park in one of the large pull-ins for cars on the Ridgeway, on either side of the B4000 Lambourn to Ashbury road, at Ashbury Hill. Follow the Ridgeway south-west on the level ride to the junction for Idstone. Turn left and follow the well-made track to

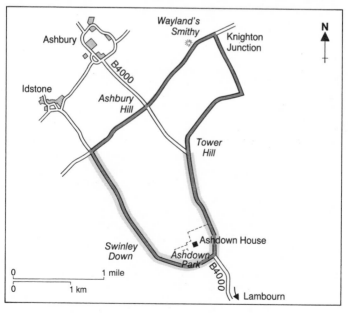

Swinley Down, and eventually to the B4000 road. Half-way along this section you will have a fine view of Ashdown House.

At the main road, turn left, and continue up the hill passing the main entrance to Ashdown Park. After a mile on this road, take the first turning to your right, a fairly well-made track heading north-east. Follow this dog-leg track through the woods, until eventually you rejoin the Ridgeway.

Turn left on the Ridgeway, passing Wayland's Smithy, until eventually you arrive back at the car park.

Facilities

Ashdown House, Lambourn, Newbury, Berkshire RG16 7RE: open April to October, Wednesday and Saturday afternoons.

FOX HILL
Pubs
Shepherd's Rest, Fox Hill, Wanborough (0793 790266).

BISHOPSTONE
Post office and general stores.
Pubs
True Heart, High Street, Bishopstone (0793 790462).
Royal Oak, Bishopstone (0793 790481).

ASHBURY
Pubs
Rose & Crown, High Street, Ashbury (079 371 222).

UFFINGTON
Attractive little village, with a fine church and a magnificent view of the White Horse and the downs.
Pubs
The Fox and Hounds, Uffington (036 782 680).
The White Horse, Broad Street, Uffington (036 782 652).

Tourist information

Faringdon: Tourist Information Centre, The Pump House, 5 Market Place, Faringdon, Oxfordshire SN7 7HL (0367 22191).

chapter 4

WHITE HORSE to GRAMPS HILL

Introduction to the area

The downs here are broad, stretching a good 5 miles to the south of the Ridgeway and providing excellent cycling conditions. Lambourn, a village 5 miles to the south, is the most famous centre for National Hunt racing in the country and the area is used intensively for the training of racehorses.

The route

Three and three-quarter miles (6 km) of the Ridgeway.
After an initial descent from White Horse Hill, there is more or less constant gradient at the 250-yd (230-m) line.
No metalled sections.

From White Horse Hill, the path drops sharply through 61 yds over 1¼ miles (56 m over 2 km). After a level section, the path drops gently again for ½ a mile (0.8 km) from Blowingstone Hill. In the dip, often very muddy, a path leads off right (south) towards Seven Barrows. As you pass Hill Barn the path is over impacted hardcore running down to a lane, where the TV mast at Eastmanton Down towers overhead. Beyond the lane the way becomes broad and grassy as it leads on to the B4001, hugging the northern lip of the downs. Just after the road on the right is the sculpted cup in the northern face of the downs called The Devil's Punchbowl. As you approach Gramps Hill the path narrows and is enclosed by thick hedges. There is often mud here.

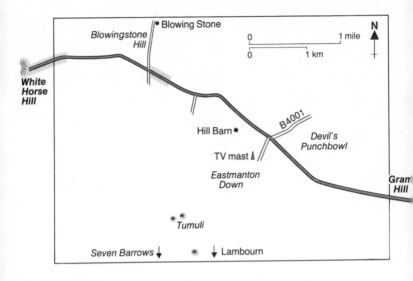

What you will see

Of all the ancient monuments on the Ridgeway the Blowing Stone, 880 yds (800 m) to the north of the Ridgeway down Blowingstone Hill, is perhaps the most curious. The waist-high stone, holed and pitted like a Gruyère, sits within a fence in the corner of a cottage garden. It is said that if one blows into the right hole a trumpeting sound can be created. King Alfred, legend has it, used it to summon his troops to battle against the Danes.

The Devil's Punchbowl is a large, natural hollow in the northern slope of the downs. A footpath leads to it from the Ridgeway and skirts the lip around to the north. From the path it is almost like looking down from an aircraft and the shadows the sun casts on the short, springy turf create the illusion that one is looking at an expanse of baked mud with the tracks of sheep like ripples in its surface.

Two miles south of the Ridgeway is Seven Barrows, a complex of Bronze Age (1800 BC – 500 BC) round and saucer barrows, or tombs. Despite the name there are many more than seven burrows in this area, perhaps as many as 40. The site, alongside the lane which leads from Blowingstone Hill to the north to Lambourn in the south, is designated an area of special scientific interest and is a nature reserve.

The rough grassland here is a rare survivor of a habitat that was once typical on the Berkshire Downs – over 100 species of plant have been identified on this 13-acre corner, which has probably never been ploughed. Plants which, before the advent of large-scale arable farming on the downs and the use of chemicals, would have been found everywhere, include Thyme, Horseshoe Vetch, Cowslips, Clustered Bellflower and Devil's-bit Scabious. Such plants attract butterflies, including the Chalkhill Blue, Small Skipper and Marbled White.

Lambourn, the only village on this section of the route, is a famous centre for National Hunt racing. The place, according to Alan Lee in his book *Lambourn, Village of Racing* (Arthur Barker 1982), is devoted entirely to the business of producing winning racehorses.

"The village is still besotted with horses," he says, "ready to throw a party, blow a week's wages and collect a mighty hangover on the strength of a local win in Saturday's big race."

In the eighteenth century racing took place at Weathercock Down to the north-west of the village, and the Red Lion Hotel, still a racing pub, was the headquarters for accepting entries.

The area was developed as a training centre by the Nugent family. Sir Hugh Nugent set up substantial gallops on the downs and, during a slump in farming in the 1920s and 1930s, encouraged landowners to convert disused farms into training centres. Today there are 40 trainers in the area, and many famous horses and jockeys.

Famous connections

Among the famous jockeys with Lambourn connections are Steve Cauthen and John Francombe. Francombe, seven times Champion Jockey and now retired, still lives nearby and now co-writes racing thrillers with James MacGregor and commentates on racing on TV.

Lambourn was the model for Marygreen in Thomas Hardy's *Jude the Obscure*. The village, Hardy says, was "as old-fashioned as it was small, and it rested in the lap of an undulating upland adjoining the North Wessex Downs".

Anyone cycling on the fine straight paths linking the village with the Ridgeway will recognise this description, though Hardy was writing in the 1890s:

Here the ploughed land ended and all before him was bleak open down . . . Not a soul was visible on the hedgeless highway, or on either side of it, and the white road seemed to ascend and diminish till it joined the sky. At the very top it was crossed at right angles by a green "ridge way" . . . this ancient track ran east and west for many miles, and down almost to within living memory had been used for driving flocks and herds to fairs and markets.

Jude and Arabella, to whom he is unhappily married, walk here on the downs:

They wandered up the slopes till they reached the green track along the ridge, which they followed to the circular British earth-bank adjoining [probably Segsbury Camp], Jude thinking of the great age of the trackway, and of the drovers who had frequented it, probably before the Romans knew the country.

Other routes

There are four or more good routes linking Lambourn with the Ridgeway which can be used as part of a circular route.

From Lambourn to the Ridgeway at Gramps Hill via Eastbury Grange: 5½ miles (8.8 km).
Ascent of 65 yds over 0.75 miles (60 m over 1.2 km) from Lambourn.
Ascent of 87 yds over 3.5 miles (80 m over 5.6 km) from Eastbury Grange to the Ridgeway.
Descent of 55 yds over 1 mile (50 m over 1.6 km) across Eastbury Down.
One and a half miles (2.4 km) on metalled roads.

Leave Lambourn travelling north on the B4001. Turn right after a few hundred yards up a lane. When the lane forks after ½ a mile (0.8 km) go right. The tarmac ends at Eastbury Down and

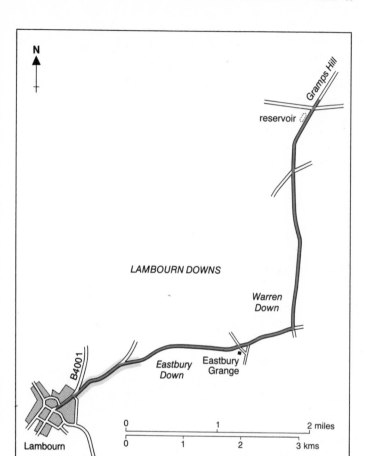

there is a smooth descent over grass, dropping 55 yds in a mile (50 m over 1.6 km).

At the foot of the hill another byway crosses the route at a T-junction just before a farm called Eastbury Grange. Keep straight on towards rising ground where two tracks ascend alongside each other. Take the less distinct path to the left. At the crossroads at the summit turn left, ascending gently on a straight farm road which stretches ahead for a mile or more.

After just under 2 miles (3.2 km) another route crosses your path. Go straight on and soon the way becomes metalled. When you see a small reservoir on your left slow down: the Ridgeway crosses your path soon after as you begin to descend the north bank of the downs and is easy to miss.

Circular route from the Ridgeway at the B4001 to Gramps Hill via Brockhampton Down: 6 miles (9.6 km).
Ascent of 33 yds over 2 miles (30 m over 3.2 km) from Brockhampton Down to Gramps Hill.
Three miles (4.8 km) on metalled roads.

From the Ridgeway travel south down the B4001 towards Lambourn. After nearly ½ a mile (0.8 km) take the narrow tarmacked farm road to the left. Signs warn this is a private road but it is designated as a byway. The road runs dead straight, descending gently, for 2 miles (3.2 km). Watch out for two

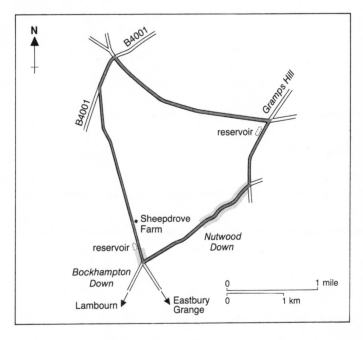

"sleeping policemen" at the only house on the route, Sheepdrove Farm.

Shortly after passing a reservoir on your left the road descends and comes to a crossroads. All routes are marked as byways here. Go left. Right would take you to Lambourn, straight ahead to Eastbury Grange.

The route descends for a mile (1.6 km) or so over tarmac, then the tarmac ends and a rough, wide track starts to climb Nutwood Down. At the T-junction turn left, reaching the Ridgeway after a few hundred yards. Turn left onto the Ridgeway and continue for 2 miles (3.2 km) back to your starting-point.

Circuit from the Ridgeway at the B4001 via Seven Barrows: 7 miles (11.2 km).

Ascent of 55 yds over ½ a mile (50 m over 0.8 km) from Seven Barrows.

Two and a third miles (3.7 km) on metalled roads.

Go west on the Ridgeway from the B4001 for just over a mile (1.6 km) until you reach a crossroads. Turn right on to a grassy, rutted path that runs dead straight downhill before joining a lane. Go straight ahead on the lane for another mile (1.6 km) until the lane swings left and a track runs off to the right.

Go right here and the track winds behind a wood and down into a valley covered with so extensive a system of gallops you feel you are in the middle of a racecourse. At a T-junction turn left. The route is marked as a byway. The path ascends between gallops for just over a mile (1.6 km) until you reach a barn on your right, where another, well-used farm track runs parallel with the route. Continue through trees for ¼ of a mile (0.4 km) until you see a block of stone, 3 feet high, to the left of the path. This is marked as Hangman's Stone on the Ordnance Survey map.

Almost immediately after Hangman's Stone turn sharp left so that you almost double back on yourself. The path descends over sharp, loose flints and then runs along the top of a field and down to a lane.

Turn left on the lane and then right, after a few hundred yards, when the lane bends left. There is a signpost here showing

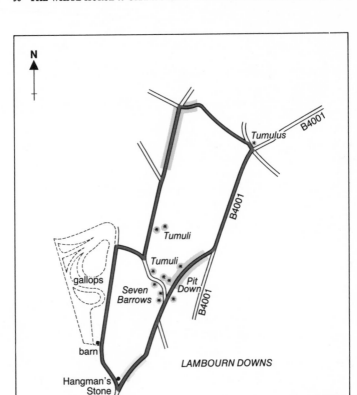

you have reached Seven Barrows. The path climbs the hill beside the site and skirts a wood before crossing Pit Down and joining the B4001. Turn left on the B-road and regain your starting-point after 1½ miles (2.4 km).

Facilities

LAMBOURN
Accommodation
The George, High Street, Lambourn (048871 289).

Pubs

The Red Lion, High Street.

The Wheelwright's Arms, The Broadway.

Food

Gino's Trattoria, High Street.

The Rice Bowl, Chinese take-away, High Street.

The Paddock, racing bistro, High Street.

The Nippy Chippy, Newbury Road.

Shops

Spar and VG supermarkets, both in High Street.

The village also has a chemist-cum-wine merchant and branches of Lloyds and Barclays banks.

Universal Stores, High Street, sells cycle repair kits and a few accessories.

Ladbrokes have a betting shop in The Broadway.

chapter 5

GRAMPS HILL to RIDGEWAY DOWN

Introduction to the area

At the mid-point of the Ridgeway the path has begun its long, gentle descent east towards the Thames at Streatley. From 762 ft (232 m) at the start of this section it falls to 657 ft (200 m) at the end of it. To the north the last substantial town before the end of the route, Wantage, is visible down on the plain.

According to Thomas Hardy, it is possible to see Oxford, 20 miles to the north, from this stretch of the Ridgeway, if conditions are right. Failing that, you might – perhaps from the ramparts of Segsbury Camp – glimpse the glinting waters of the Thames, 12 miles away.

The twin villages of Letcombe Bassett and Letcombe Regis, in the shadow of the downs to the north, are worth a detour.

The route

Four and a half miles (2.8 km) of the Ridgeway.
No substantial ascents or descents.
One mile (1.6 km) on metalled road.

For the first mile (1.6 km) the path descends gently. This stretch, which is fairly narrow, is often very muddy. Because the path is enclosed by hawthorn bushes there are no grassy verges on which to escape the mud. There then follows an equally gentle climb for ½ a mile (0.8 km) which brings you to the junction with the A338.

Turn right on the main road, which fortunately is neither too wide nor too busy, and then left after a few yards onto the continuation of the Ridgeway.

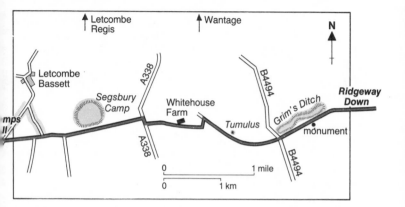

Here the path runs on a metalled farm road past Whitehouse Farm before turning sharp left and then right. The tarmac ends and the Ridgeway continues over earth to its junction with the B4494 Newbury to Wantage road. The section finishes with a smooth descent over grass past a memorial to Lord Wantage.

What you will see

Half a mile (0.8 km) west of the A338 is the Iron Age fort of Segsbury Camp, also known as Letcombe Castle. All that is visible now are a shallow ditch and a rampart covered in hawthorn bushes encircling 26 acres of hill-top. The fort is planted with crops and bisected by a lane.

When the site was excavated in 1871 a good deal of Iron Age pottery was found, along with human bones in a cist, flint scrapers and a Saxon shield boss. Until at least the eighteenth century the rampart was faced with sarsen stones.

Today the fort is obscured and perhaps unimpressive, but its commanding position still makes clear what great strategic importance it would once have had. It is just yards from the historically vital supply route of the Ridgeway.

To the north, Wantage is in its protective shadow, as is the network of routes which feed in to the town. In particular, it overlooks the intersection of the north/south A338 and the east/west A417, both ancient, important routes.

Wantage, 3 miles (4.8 km) to the north of the Ridgeway, was the birthplace of King Alfred, ruler of southern England, in AD 849. Although his capital was at Winchester, he probably once had a palace in or near the town, although no sign of it survives. There is a Victorian statue of him, however, in the market square. Alfred founded the Royal Navy and, reputedly, the University of Oxford.

A few hundred yards east of the junction with the B4494 is a monument to Robert Lloyd-Lindsay, Baron Wantage, founder of the British Red Cross Society and a distinguished soldier, who won the Victoria Cross in the Crimean War.

He had a substantial estate on the downs and, through the planting of scattered copses and belts of trees designed to give shelter to livestock and crops, had a strong influence over the modern-day appearance of the landscape.

Famous connections

Letcombe Bassett was the model for Cresscombe in Thomas Hardy's *Jude the Obscure*. It is to this stretch of the Ridgeway that the young Jude comes to gaze north towards Christminster (Oxford).

Looking across the northern plain just before sunset he discovered that:

Some way within the limits of the stretch of landscape, points of light like topaz gleamed. The air increased in transparency with the lapse of minutes, till the topaz points showed themselves to be the vanes, windows, wet roof slates, and other shining spots upon the spires, domes, freestone-work and varied outlines that were faintly revealed. It was Christminster, unquestionably; either directly seen, or miraged in the peculiar atmosphere.

Jude is passing through Cresscombe on his way to Marygreen (Lambourn) to the south of the downs when he meets Arabella Donn, with whom he shares a short disastrous marriage. The description of how he reaches her "isolated house, in the dip beyond the upland" pinpoints the location: "descending the steep side of the country . . . he neared the brook that oozed from it, and followed the stream till he reached her dwelling".

It is along this stream, between the villages of Letcombe
Bassett and Letcombe Regis, that the shallow watercress beds,
for which the village was once famous, have been created. The
cottage still stands isolated among the watercress.

Jonathan Swift, author of *Gulliver's Travels*, lived in Letcombe
Bassett from June to September 1714. He was a friend of the
vicar and stayed at the Rectory. He wrote *Free Thoughts on the
Present State of Affairs* and *Verses on Himself* in the village, and
was visited by Alexander Pope.

Other routes

Circuit from Letcombe Bassett via the Ridgeway and Letcombe Regis: 4 miles (6.4 km).

Ascent of 100 yds over 1 mile (110 m over 1.6 km) from Letcombe
Bassett to the Ridgeway.

Three miles (4.8 km) on metalled roads.

From Letcombe Bassett village take the lane signposted "Downs
and Church". At the Y-junction take the left fork. At the summit

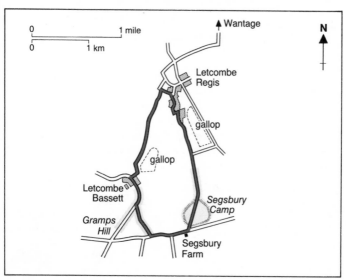

the route joins the Ridgeway at a T-junction. Turn left. Turn left again after ½ a mile (0.8 km), opposite the entrance to Segsbury Farm. The route runs through the middle of Segsbury Camp, becoming metalled after a few hundred yards.

Carry straight on down the lane until you reach Letcombe Regis. Follow the road as it turns first sharp left and then, immediately afterwards, sharp right. At the crossroads carry straight on, passing to the right of the church. Follow the lane as it turns sharp left and climbs gently uphill. To your left is the narrow, steeply sided valley in which Letcombe Brook runs. A mile (1.6 km) out of Letcombe Regis the road dips down into the valley and crosses the river before climbing again up into Letcombe Bassett.

Circuit from Wantage via the Ridgeway, Court Hill Ridgeway Centre and Letcombe Regis: 8 miles (12.8 km).
Ascent of 200 yds over 2 miles (220 m over 3.2 km) from Wantage to the Ridgeway.
Five miles (8 km) on metalled roads.

Leave Wantage travelling west on the B4507. After ½ a mile (0.8 km) take the lane on the left signposted to Letcombe Regis. At the crossroads in the village centre turn right, keeping the church on your left, following a sign to Letcombe Bassett.

In this village take the road to the left signposted "Downs and Church". At the Y-junction take the right fork. After ½ a mile (0.8 km) the lane crosses the Ridgeway. Turn left on the Ridgeway, heading east. Follow the route for about 3½ miles (5.6 km). After 1½ miles (2.4 km) the route crosses the A338.

Turn right onto this road then left after a few yards. Both turns are signposted. Continue along the farm lane for ½ a mile (0.8 km) and follow it as it turns sharp left and then sharp right. Here the tarmac stops. After ¼ of a mile (0.4 km) is a Y-junction. The Ridgeway continues on the left-hand fork. The very similar-looking route to the right takes you to Farnborough (details later in this chapter).

After ½ a mile (0.8 km) the route crosses the B4494. The way descends gently over grass. Shortly after the memorial to Lord

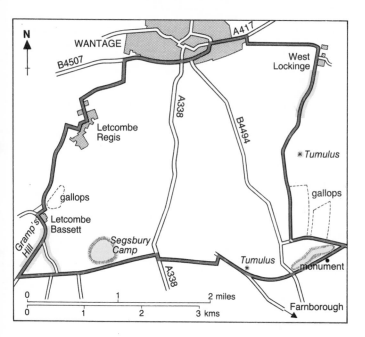

Wantage take the track doubling back down to the left and running alongside a wood. When the road enters the wood take the bridleway, which is signposted, just to the right. The path follows the road within the belt of trees.

After a few hundred yards the lane swings right and cuts across your path. Cross the road heading for the open country directly ahead. You emerge on a farm track with the open downs to your left and a gallop to the right. The route runs along the top of the gallop and then follows it around to the right. Keep to the left of the gallop as you descend the hill towards West Lockinge.

Once beyond the gallops the path becomes a cinder track running downhill between trees. After a cattle grid, and a haybarn to your right, you are running downhill in a narrow fold in the downs.

After a second cattle grid the path levels out and, after a third grid, runs straight through a farmyard and out into a lane. Turn left. The lane swings left and runs between an avenue of trees. When it turns sharp right take the path going straight ahead. The path ends at a road. Turn right. After a few yards you meet the A417. Turn left to go back into Wantage town centre.

Circuit from the Ridgeway over the southern downs via South Fawley: 10.5 miles (16.8 km).
No notable ascents or descents.
Half a mile (0.8 km) on metalled roads.

The route begins on the Ridgeway where it is crossed by the A338. There is room to park to the west of the main road. Follow the Ridgeway, travelling west for just under a mile (0.8 km) before turning left a couple of hundred yards after Segsbury Farm.

The path runs dead straight and almost due south for 2 miles (3.2 km). A mile (1.6 km) after leaving the Ridgeway you come

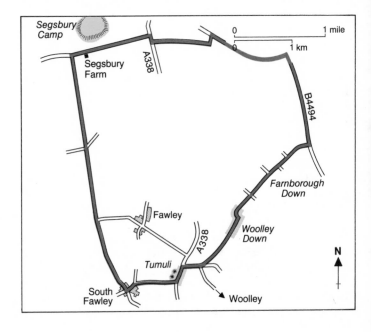

to where a farm lane crosses the route. Go straight on. After a further ½ a mile or so (0.8 km) the route is tarmacked for a short section. When the metalled route swings off to the left to Fawley, go straight on, across cornfields. An Ordnance Survey triangulation station marks the route.

After a mile (1.6 km) the path runs through a farm and joins a lane. This is South Fawley. Turn right on the lane which first dips and then climbs up to the A338. Turn left on the A-road and, after a few hundred yards, right. There is a war memorial at the junction, and a signpost for Woolley.

The lane descends before turning right at a wood. Take the wide, hardcore-covered route to the left, keeping the trees to your right. The path soon reverts to grass and narrows to vehicle width.

There are two ruined cottages to the right and a gallop to the left as you ascend Woolley Down. Three-quarters of a mile (1.2 km) up this path the route dog-legs to left and then right around an area of rough grassland, exiting via a narrow break in the fence marked on either side by a bush.

The path runs fairly straight for a mile (1.6 km), but the surface changes several times as farm roads join and leave it. A quarter of a mile (0.4 km) on, at Farnborough Downs, there are routes to left and right. Go straight on across a short stretch of concrete then through woods before reaching the B4494.

Turn left and follow it for just over a mile (1.6 km) until the Ridgeway crosses it. Turn left onto the Ridgeway, travelling west, and follow it for 1½ miles (2.4 km) until you reach the A338. (For further details on this section of the route refer to the description of the Ridgeway at the start of this chapter.)

From the Ridgeway to Farnborough: 3 miles (4.8 km).
A gentle descent.
Negligible stretch on metalled road.

(This route can be tacked on to any of the above rides except the Letcombe Bassett circuit. Farnborough is also easily accessible from the Southern Downs circuit described in the previous chapter.)

If you are cycling the Ridgeway from east to west it is easiest

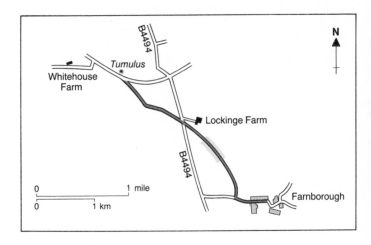

to approach the village from the east and then reverse the route outlined here to regain the Ridgeway to the west of the village.

If you are cycling from west to east follow the description here to reach the village and regain the Ridgeway to the east by first following the lane from Farnborough towards West Ilsley, turning left after 1½ miles (2.4 km) by a house called Lands End. Here a path leads up West Ginge Down to the Ridgeway.)

The bridleway to Farnborough leaves the Ridgeway, travelling south-east, at a Y-junction ½ a mile (0.8 km) west of the B4494. Take the right fork. You are on a narrow path running among trees. After a mile (1.6 km) the path comes out on the B4494.

According to the Ordnance Survey map the route should cut across the road at an angle and continue on the same path towards the village. In fact you must turn right on to the road and then left after a few yards into the drive to Lockinge Kiln Farm. Skirt the yard, keeping right, and you come out in a field.

Turn right, keeping to the edge of the field, and you soon see the path to Farnborough running off to the left between high hedges. The path continues straight on for 1¼ miles (2 km). It is less well used than most bridleways and overgrown in summer. When the path meets a lane turn left. You are at the outskirts of the village.

Facilities

WANTAGE

A pleasant market town with a Georgian centre and a fine market square. It has a full range of shops, including a cycle shop, banks, cafes, several pubs and hotels.

Accommodation

The Bear Hotel, Market Place, Wantage, Oxon (02357 66366). Weekend breaks at special rates. Restaurant open seven days for breakfast, lunch and dinner.

The Royal Oak Inn, Newbury Street (02357 3129).

Cycle sales and repairs

Wantage Motorcycles, Church Street, Wantage (02357 68643).

Accommodation close to the Ridgeway

The YHA Court Hill Ridgeway Centre is just north of the Ridgeway where it is crossed by the A338. As well as conventional youth hostel accommodation it has four-berth cabins with washing facilities and two holiday flats.

The centre was created from five timber-framed buildings brought to the site and is very attractive. There is an open-air swimming pool. For bookings contact The Warden, Court Hill, Letcombe Regis, nr Wantage, Oxon. (02357 60253).

LETCOMBE REGIS
Pubs
The Sparrow (02357 3228).
The Greyhound (02357 3023).

LETCOMBE BASSETT
Pubs
The Yew Tree (02357 3140).

chapter 6

RIDGEWAY DOWN to THE A34

Introduction to the area

The downs are becoming progressively narrower as the gentle descent to the Thames at Streatley continues, but there is still a good 3-mile belt of fine cycling country to the south of the Ridgeway, and up to 1½ miles to the north. The area is sparsely populated, with just one small village, West Ilsley, close to the route.

West Ilsley is a racing village, with a substantial racing stable – owned by the Queen – and two stretches of gallops running up to the summit of the downs to the east and west of the village. While the ride along the Ridgeway itself gives fantastic views over the plains to the north, the circular routes from West Ilsley described later in this chapter take full advantage of the fine, rolling land to the south.

The route

Four and a quarter miles (7 km) of the Ridgeway.
No notable ascents or descents.
No metalled stretches.

The path runs along the northern lip of the downs. For all of this stretch the route is 40 ft wide and grassy, with an often muddy vehicle track winding along to one side of it.

Except for a narrow lane meeting the route from the north just east of Scutchamer Knob there are no vehicle access points until Bury Down, where there is a large car park. To the north the lane meets the A34. The Ridgeway is signposted from the main road, and this is a busy spot. West Ilsley is 1½ miles south.

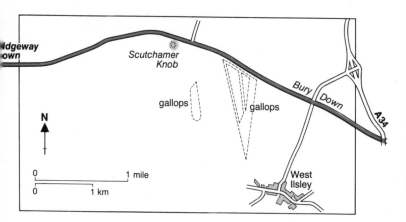

What you will see

One and a half miles (2.4 km) west of Ridgeway Down is a horseshoe-shaped earth rampart called Scutchamer Knob. It is in a wood just to the south of the path. There are at least two theories about what the Knob might be.

One view is that it is an Iron Age barrow (burial chamber) which was later used by the Saxons as a burial and meeting place. The name, according to this theory, comes from *Cwichelm-shlaew*, meaning burial place of Cwichelm, who was a Saxon king of Wessex and died in 593 AD.

The Anglo-Saxon Chronicle recounts a story of a raid which the Saxons carried out, in 1006, from their safe haven on the Isle of Wight against the Danes, who held the land to the north of the Ridgeway:

They went to Wallingford and burned it to the ground and proceeded along the Berkshire Downs to Cuckhamsley Knob and there awaited the great things that had been threatened, for it had often been said that if ever they got as far as Cuckhamsley Knob, they would never again reach the sea, but they went back by another route.

Another theory is that the name comes from the word "scutcher". A scutcher was a man who beat out, or scutched, the wettened flax which was the raw material for cloth. The Ginge Brook, which flows between the nearby villages of West Ginge and East Ginge, powered mills in which the flax was beaten prior to scutching. The Knob, this theory goes, was the place where the villagers, most of whom would have been employed in the cloth industry, held festivities.

West Ilsley is one of the most famous racing villages on the downs. At the Queen's West Ilsley Stables, at Hodcott House, just to the east of the village, over 100 horses are in training at any one time, about a dozen of them likely to belong to the monarch. Until autumn 1990 the trainer was Dick Hearn.

In his 22 years at West Ilsley Major Hearn prepared an extraordinary succession of horses to win every major prize in the sport. In the 1988 season, for example, he helped train the winners of 41 races with prize money of £500,000. His place at the stables was taken by Will Hastings-Bass.

Around 50 people, a very large proportion of this tiny community, earn their living from training racehorses. The village's life focuses on the stable, which is something of a village-within-a-village. Among famous champions trained here were the Queen's Highclere, which won the 1,000 Guineas and French Oaks in 1974, Dunfermline, which won the Oaks and St Leger three years later, and Minster Son, another St Leger winner. There have been stables here since 1840.

Famous connections

John and Penelope Betjeman loved this section of the Ridgeway and often walked it. They lived at Farnborough, the next village west from West Ilsley. John Piper designed a window in the village church in memory of Betjeman.

An inscription on a plaque beneath the predominantly green and blue window, in which fish, butterflies and a plant bearing all kinds of fruit are depicted, reads:

In memory of Sir John Betjeman, 1906–1984, Poet Laureate, sometime resident at the Old Rectory, Farnborough. This window, designed by his friend John Piper, and executed by Joseph Nuttgens, was placed here by the Friends of Friendless Churches. I am the Resurrection and the Life.

There is a memorial to Penelope on the Ridgeway itself. You will find it, perhaps with difficulty, a mile west of Scutchamer Knob where a bridleway crosses the path.

Penelope was a keen horsewoman and often rode on the downs. Her daughter Candida commemorated her connection in 1987 when she had a small sarsen stone, bearing a plaque, placed on the edge of Lockinge Estate, just beyond a small wood to the north of the path. The simple inscription reads: "In memory of Penelope Betjeman (1910–1986) who loved The Ridgeway".

Edward Thomas, the poet and journalist killed in the First World War (see chapter 2), explored the Ridgeway in 1910. Approaching from the east, he felt he had reached the real, unsullied path when he got to this stretch. He wrote of it:

Now the Ridgeway had risen up to its perfect freedom, away from the river and the low land, from the glaring roads and the collections of houses. This way men of old came from necessity; yet I found it hard not to think now that the road was thus climbing to heights of speculation, to places suited for exploring the ridges and solitudes of the spirit; it seemed in one mood a hermit road going out of the wilderness to meditate and be in lifelong retirement; in another mood a road for the young, eager warrior or reformer going up and away for a time from cloying companions to renew his mighty youth.

Other routes

Circuit from West Ilsley via Bury Down: 4½ miles (7.2 km).
Ascent of 55 yds over 1 mile (60 m over 1.6 km) from West Ilsley.
Half a mile (0.8 km) on metalled roads.

Leave West Ilsley heading east and take the first path to the left, signposted "Cart Track". The track runs straight uphill with woodland on the right after a few hundred yards. Once you are past the trees the gallops of Hodcott Down appear, also on the right.

Turn left on to the Ridgeway, crossing the lane at Bury Down and continuing for another 1¼ miles (1.9 km). The right turn back to the village is hard to spot and care needs to be taken to identify it correctly. At East Hendred Down look out for two bridleways joining the Ridgeway from the north within a few yards of each other.

Your path is on the left immediately after them and marked at its start by two substantial, square, white-painted posts. A

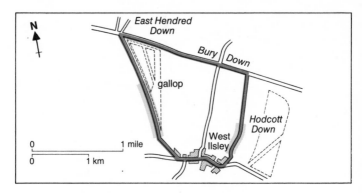

gallop runs alongside the Ridgeway at this point. Ride straight across it and turn left to follow the fence on the other side.

While one gallop stretches back alongside the Ridgeway, the other peels off downhill. Follow the latter. An indistinct earth path runs along on the left-hand side of this gallop. The Hendred Estate has placed several signs warning against trespassing at this point, but nothing to help the rider identify his route.

The path soon becomes more distinct and provides a smooth, fast descent to the village. Turn left at the lane to regain your starting-point.

Circuit from West Ilsley via the Ridgeway and the southern downs: 11.5 miles (18.5 km).
Ascent of 65 yds over 1 mile (60 m over 1.6 km), from the village to the Ridgeway. Ascent of 65 yds over 1½ miles (60 m over 2.4 km) from Lands End.
Descent of 65 yds over 1¼ miles (60 m over 1.6 km) from Ridgeway Down.
No metalled roads.

Leave West Ilsley heading east and take the first path left, signposted "Cart Track". Turn left onto the Ridgeway crossing the lane at Bury Down and reaching East Hendred Down after 1 mile (1.6 km). Another 2 miles (3.2 km) brings you to Ridgeway Down.

With the path dipping down and the memorial to Lord Wantage just visible ahead, look for a path on the right, just

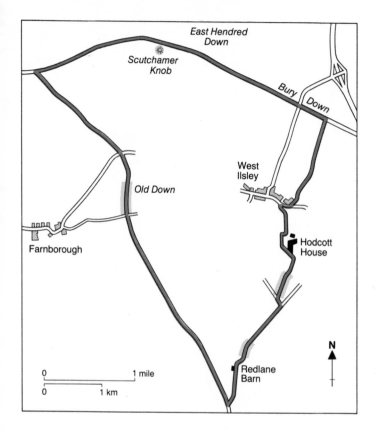

before a belt of straggly bushes, onto Wether Down.

The fine soft turf here, ridged by the hooves of countless horses, causes the bike's tyres to set up a gentle drumming. The woods on either side of the belt of open ground we follow had their hearts ripped out in the storms of 1990. Carry straight on until the path crosses a lane beside a house at Lands End.

You now climb up Old Down on a path which begins at vehicle width but quickly narrows as you reach woodland. (Just after you enter the woods a path to the left offers a diversion to Farnborough, John Betjeman's former home, a mile (1.6 km) away.)

Carry straight on through the woods until you reach another lane. Turn right and follow it for a couple of hundred yards looking for a gate into a field on the left. Go into the field, turning immediately right inside it to follow the path that runs dead ahead through two fields and into a wood.

After ¼ of a mile (0.4 km) the wood thins to a narrow band of trees on your left. After a break in the trees on your left you reach a Y-junction. Turn left. The route runs between fields and past a small farm called Redlane Barn. Turn left immediately past the house. You are now heading back to West Ilsley. Take the right fork at the woods, where the path divides, and you come out into a field. Continue down its left-hand side.

The path sweeps downhill, giving a good view for miles ahead along a fold in the downs. Just peeping over the horizon is the tip of the tallest chimney at Didcot Power Station.

After ¾ of a mile (1.2 km) you reach a five-barred gate. Go through it and continue straight on until a signpost denotes a fork in the path. Turn left here, marked "Bridleway". Right, marked "Byway", would take you the 1½ miles (2.4 km) to East Ilsley.

After 100 yards (110 m) down a steep hill, turn right and follow the grassy path as it sweeps round to the left in an arc, with the rooftops of West Ilsley becoming visible. At a crossroads go as near to straight ahead as you can, on a path marked "Bridleway". The route skirts Hodcott House before joining a lane. Turn left and follow the lane back into West Ilsley.

Facilities

WEST ILSLEY
Accommodation
The Harrow (063528 260).
The pub does meals and welcomes children.
Shops
The Village Stores, which sells a range of food and drink, is in the main street in the centre of the village.
The Post Office is at the eastern end of the main street.

FARNBOROUGH
No facilities.

chapter 7

THE A34 to
RODEN DOWNS

Introduction to the area

After so many miles of solitude and unmarred beauty, the twentieth century begins to intrude again on this stretch of the Ridgeway.

The roar of the A34, beneath which the route passes in a concrete tunnel, combines with the eyesores, on the northern plain, of the Harwell Laboratory and the six giant cooling towers of Didcot Power Station to make this the only unattractive spot along the route.

Once away from the road things improve. For the first half of the section, the path runs along the lip of the downs, giving views north which are impressive, despite the blemishes, before swinging left and becoming engulfed by softly contoured hills which stretch away to the horizon on either side.

On Roden Downs is an intersection that could not be more rural. Paths to Aldworth, Compton and Blewbury all converge here on the Ridgeway itself.

East Ilsley and Compton give good access to this stretch of the route.

The route

From the A34 to Roden Downs: 3½ miles (5.6 km) of the Ridgeway.
Descent of 50 yds over 1 mile (45 m over 1.6 km) from Several Down to the course of the railway at Blewbury Down.

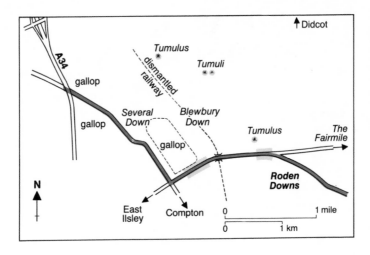

Ascent of 40 yds over ½ a mile (35 m over 0.8 km) to the east of Roden Downs.
Quarter of a mile (0.4 km) on metalled road.

From the A34 the path runs on the level, with gallops to north and south before, at Several Down, joining a single-track concrete farm road which drops gently for ½ a mile (0.8 km). At the crossroads (signposted) turn left (north-east) to continue along the Ridgeway. Straight on (south-east) would take you to Compton and right (south-west) to East Ilsley.

The path descends over grass, dropping 50 yds in 1 mile (45 m over 1.6 km), to cross the course of a dismantled railway before a climb of 40 yds in the space of ⅓ of a mile (35 m over 0.5 km).

At the Y-junction just before Roden Downs be sure to take the right fork. The left takes you on to The Fair Mile, which descends to the A417 to the north of Streatley. The final ½ mile (0.8 km) to Roden Downs is over level ground.

What you will see

On the Ridgeway just east of the A34 there is a memorial stone to a soldier. The inscription reads:

Hugh Frederick Grosvenor
Second Lieutenant the Life Guards
lost his life in an armoured car accident while on military duty
9th April 1947   Aged 19 years

It makes you glad not to have had to navigate the A34, though a trip through the tunnel makes you aware that even the Ridgeway is not free of graffiti. A multicoloured scrawl on the wall of the underpass told us that the Agro Crue 88 had discovered its pleasures before us.

In the valley to the north are the six giant cooling towers of Didcot Power Station and the sprawling mass of the Harwell Laboratory, formerly the Atomic Energy Research Establishment. But the cooling towers do not always look ugly. Sometimes, in the early morning, with a mist covering the valley floor, they seem to float eerily, and rather impressively, in space.

The course of a dismantled railway, the former Didcot, Newbury and Southampton line, crosses the Ridgeway at Blewbury Down. There was once a station in Compton. Kenneth Grahame, the author of *The Wind in the Willows* and a one-time resident of Blewbury, to the east, knew the line when it was still operational and said of it: "Out on that almost trackless expanse of billowy Downs such a track is in some sort humanly companionable; it really seems to lead you by the hand."

East Ilsley, to the south of the Ridgeway, was once called Market Ilsley and was the site of an important sheep fair. Sheep were driven here, along the Ridgeway and the network of upland tracks, from as far away as Salisbury. From 1620 fairs were held once or twice a month and the last took place in 1934.

Farmers came here from throughout southern England and there were 13 pubs to cater for them. There are still three, quite a number for a village of just a few dozen houses.

During the eighteenth century there were also huge annual fairs at which 80,000 sheep changed hands. The downs declined as a lamb-breeding area when competition from New Zealand became strong. In the 1970s there were attempts to revive the fairs, but they failed, and today you are more likely to see cattle on the downs than sheep.

Half-way up the hill towards East Ilsley's church is a grassy field and, across the road, a notice identifying this as the old market place.

When sheep ceased to be a money-spinner, racehorses took their place. William Augustus, Duke of Cumberland and second son of George II, who founded the course and meetings at Ascot, built a training stables at East Ilsley, and began a tradition which still thrives.

Other routes in the area

Circular route from Compton via the Ridgeway: 4½ miles (7.2 km).

Ascent of 42 yds over 2 miles (40 m over 3.2 km) from Compton. No metalled roads.

In Compton take the lane beside the Swan Hotel then, as it swings left after a couple of hundred yards, turn right into Wallingford Road. Turn right and pass under the old railway and turn immediately right again on to a narrow path over grass.

The route swings left and proceeds between hedges, climbing

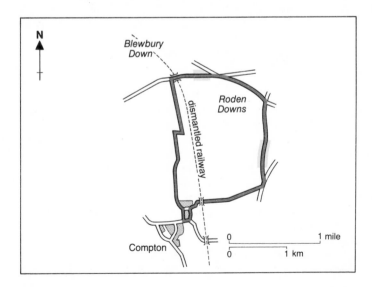

gently until, after a mile (1.6 km), it joins a chalk farm track. Turn left here and keep left at the Y-junction you come across shortly. The mile (1.6 km) before you meet the Ridgeway at Roden Downs is fast and smooth, but is heavily used by farm machinery and can be rutted and very muddy.

Turn left on to the Ridgeway. Keep left at the Y-junction you meet after ½ a mile (0.8 km) and turn left on the path immediately after you have crossed the old railway bridge. You now have a descent of 1½ miles (2.4 km) back to Compton on a route which is also used as a gallop.

The wide, grassy path complete with the white, single-board fencing seen at racecourses can make you feel more like a jockey in the saddle than a cyclist. Coming off the downs the route joins a narrow lane leading down to the main road. Turn left here and you are just a few yards from your starting-point.

Circular route from Compton via Blewbury: 11 miles (17.7 km). Ascent of 44 yds over 2 miles (40 m over 3.2 km) from Compton. Ninety yds over ¾ of a mile (80 m over 1.2 km) from the A417. Six and a half miles (8.8 km) on metalled roads.

In Compton take the lane beside the Swan Hotel then, as it swings left after a couple of hundred yards, turn right into Wallingford Road. Turn right and pass under the old railway and turn immediately right again on to a narrow path over grass.

The route swings left and proceeds between hedges, climbing gently until, after a mile (1.6 km), it joins a chalk farm track. Turn left here and keep left at the Y-junction you come across shortly. The mile (1.6 km) before you meet the Ridgeway at Roden Downs is fast and smooth, but is heavily used by farm machinery and can be rutted and very muddy. When you meet the Ridgeway go straight across.

The route continues straight ahead for 2 miles (3.2 km) until reaching the A417 at Blewbury. Turn left on to the main A417.

At the other end of the village take a left turn on to a narrow lane. Follow it for 2½ very flat miles (3.2 km) until you meet the course of a dismantled railway. Turn right, cross the railway and then take the left fork at the Y-junction just after it.

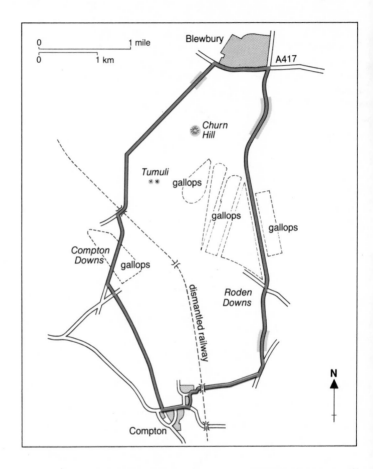

Cross extensive and complex gallops on Compton Downs until you reach a concrete road. Turn left onto the road. Very shortly it crosses the Ridgeway and then runs gently downhill for 1½ miles (2.4 km) to Compton. Turn left at the bottom of the lane to get back to your starting-point.

This is perhaps the flattest of all crossings of the downs.

Note: If you like acrobatics, there is a good spot close to Blewbury. Take the path marked "Bridleway" which travels south from the western extremity of the village. A narrow, steep path winds between thorny bushes and climbs through 90 yds over ¾ of a mile (80 m over 1.2 km) to an old quarry, just before the summit of Churn Hill. The 50-yd circumference of the quarry is criss-crossed with paths. This is not a bad place to put a mountain bike through its paces.

Circular route from Compton to East Ilsley: 4½ miles (7.2 km).
Ascent of 50 yds in 1½ miles (45 in 2.4 km) from leaving Compton.
Two miles (3.2 km) on metalled roads.

Take the first right (when facing west) after the Swan Hotel. After passing to the right of the Agricultural Research Council's Field Station the lane ends and the route continues north over grass on a gallop.

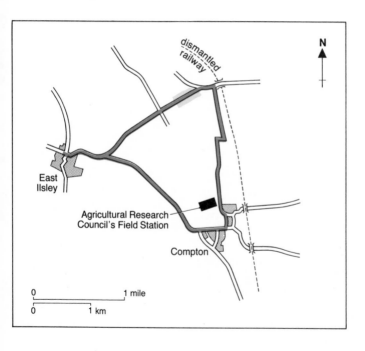

When the path reaches the Ridgeway turn left and bear left at the Y-junction you come across after a few yards. After ½ a mile (0.8 km) there is a signposted crossroads. Go straight on, signposted to East Ilsley. There is a descent over grass for ¾ of a mile (1.2 km) to a lane. Turn right on the lane for East Ilsley village or, if you wish to return directly to Compton, go left. Compton is 2 miles (3.2 km) away along a normally quiet road.

Circuit from East Ilsley via the Ridgeway: 2½ miles (4 km).
Ascent of 32 yds over 1 mile (30 m over 1.6 km) from East Ilsley. Negligible stretch on metalled roads.

Take the bridleway which leaves the lane for Compton just to the east of the village. It runs parallel to a gallop and is heavily used by horses. Though the surface is usually dry and the ascent to the Ridgeway a gentle one, the path is heavily pitted.

Follow the bridleway for a mile or so (1.6 km) until you reach the Ridgeway. Turn left and almost immediately left again, for the descent back to the village.

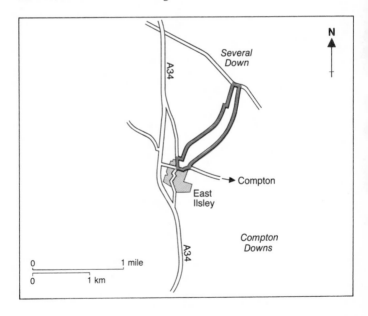

Circuit from East Ilsley via the Ridgeway and Bury Down: 6 miles (9.6 km).
Ascent of 55 yds over ½ a mile (50 m over 0.8 km) from the A34. One and a half miles (2.4 km) on metalled roads.

Leave East Ilsley on the lane to Compton. Take the turning on the left after just under ½ a mile (0.8 km) from East Ilsley. Take the bridleway to the left after a further ½ a mile (0.8 km). After a few hundred yards the path crosses the Ridgeway.

Go straight on, crossing Compton Downs, until you arrive at a bridge over a dismantled railway. Turn left before the railway and follow a straight, level track running parallel to its course.

You are cycling along the foot of the downs, which from here look gentle and low. Way up ahead to the north-west the narrow, snaking white line of the Ridgeway can be seen climbing up over the higher country described in previous chapters.

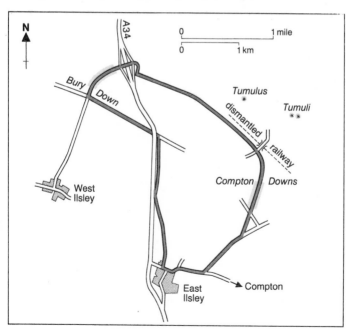

After a mile (1.6 km) the track switches from earth to hardcore and becomes a boneshaker. After 1½ miles (2.4 km) you come to the A34. Turn right on to the tarmacked road and then left at a mini-roundabout to cross the bridge. Follow the lane on the other side, over another roundabout, signposted to West Ilsley.

You now have a 55-yd climb over ½ a mile (50 m over 0.8 km) to reach the Ridgeway at Bury Down. There are large car parks here and the path is a good 40 feet wide. To return to East Ilsley turn left and follow the Ridgeway under the A34. Turn first right after emerging from it and a track takes you parallel with the A34 down to its feed-off to East Ilsley. Join the road here and follow it into the village.

Alternatively, if you are cycling along the Ridgeway from east to west, turn right when you meet the path at Bury Down.

Facilities

EAST ILSLEY
Accommodation
The Crown and Horns (0635 28205).
Other pubs
The Star (0635 28215).
The Swan (0635 28238).

COMPTON
Pubs
The Red Lion (0635 578370).
The Swan (0635 578269).
Shops
The Village Stores.
Post Office.

chapter 8

RODEN DOWNS to STREATLEY

Introduction to the area

The last four miles of the Ridgeway take you from the remote
hill-top crossroads at Roden Downs to the quaint Thames-side
villages of Goring and Streatley.

The route is swift and smooth and, with the superb views
ahead over the Thames Valley, deep into Oxfordshire and over
the Chiltern hills, a fitting end to the journey. The Ridgeway here
drops down to the gorge, known as the Goring Gap, which the
Thames has cut through the chalk downs.

If you are cycling from east to west, starting from Streatley,
what is notable is the speed with which you leave civilisation
behind and attain the solitude of the downs. From an inauspi-
cious start winding along what seems like just any old country
lane past solid, red-brick Victorian villas and a golf course, the
Ridgeway suddenly shrugs off suburbia and cuts an unwavering
line straight on, up to the top of the hills and the longest, most
sustained wilderness route in southern England.

Blewbury and Aldworth also provide good access points to this
end of the Ridgeway.

The route

The last 4 miles (6.4 km) of the Ridgeway.
Ascent of 45 yds over ½ a mile (40 m over 0.8 km) from Roden
Downs to Warren Farm.
Descent through 150 yds over 3¼ miles (140 m over 5.1 km) from
Warren Farm to Streatley.
A mile and a half (2.4 km) on metalled roads.

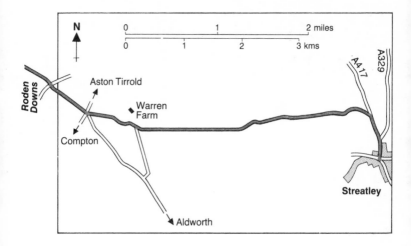

A quarter of a mile (0.4 km) after beginning the gentle ascent east over grass from Roden Downs a bridleway crosses the path. To the right (south-west) it leads to Compton, to the left (north-east) to Aston Tirrold.

Shortly afterwards is a Y-junction. Take the left fork. Right leads to Aldworth. Parallel with Warren Farm the descent, over firm chalk, to Streatley begins. After 1½ miles (2.4 km) the way becomes tarmacked, descending for the same distance again to the A417. Turn right and, at the junction with the A329, right again.

What you will see

Man has forded the Thames at Streatley for millennia, and the relative ease of the crossing here accounts for the Ridgeway's descent at this point. Although the Romans shunned the upland Ridgeway in favour of their own lines of communication on lower ground close to water, they too forded the river here.

During the ninth century, the river delineated the Saxon kingdom of Wessex to the south and west of the Thames which was held by King Alfred, born further along the Ridgeway's route at Wantage. Across the river to the north was the kingdom of the Danish Vikings.

The most easterly of the forts which once guarded the Ridgeway is at Blewburton Hill, just to the east of Blewbury, and can be reached from the village along a bridleway. Although this fort is 2 miles north of the Ridgeway, those further west are close to the route.

When the fort was excavated, the remains of grain pits, apparently a garrison's store, were discovered. The fort does not seem to have been used by the Romans, but the Saxons had a cemetery here and, presumably, a settlement.

Aldworth, a couple of miles south of the Ridgeway, has an ancient monument of a different kind. At the church, St Mary's, is one of the finest collections of fourteenth-century stone-effigies in the country. The nine effigies, which commemorate members of the de la Beche family, lords of the local manor, were defaced by Puritans in the 1650s.

Famous connections

Aldworth has been home to a pair of modern humorists. The cartoonist Osbert Lancaster lived here in a small cottage with his wife Anne until his death in 1985 at the age of 77. He was best known for the pocket cartoons he drew in the *Daily Express* from 1939. He was a great friend of John Betjeman, who also had strong Ridgeway connections.

Richard Ingrams, the former editor of *Private Eye*, still lives in Aldworth, and occasionally plays the organ in the parish church.

Blewbury was the retirement home of Kenneth Grahame, creator of *The Wind in the Willows*. He moved to a thatched farmhouse called Bohams in 1910 and lived there for 14 years. While he lived in Blewbury his only son, an undergraduate at Oxford, was killed in a train accident. Grahame, convinced it was suicide and unable to endure the connections Blewbury had after this, moved away.

Kenneth Grahame was a nature-worshipper. He loved the Ridgeway and walked on it for miles almost daily. In *The Pagan Papers*, published in 1898, he said this of the most easterly stretch of the route:

Join it at Streatley, the point where it crosses the Thames; at once it strikes you out and away from the habitable world in a splendid purposeful manner, running along the highest ridge of the Downs, a broad green ribbon of turf . . . No villages nor homesteads tempt it aside or modify its course for a yard; should you lose the track where it is blent with the bordering turf or merged in and obliterated by criss-cross paths you have only to walk straight on, taking heed of no alternative to right or left; and in a minute 'tis with you again – risen out of the earth as it were. Or, if still not quite assured, lift you your eyes, and there it runs over the brow of the fronting hill.

Blewbury was also home, in the eighteenth century, to a famous miser. The Reverend Morgan Jones, the village curate, became the model for Blackberry Jones in Charles Dickens' *Our Mutual Friend*.

Other routes in the area

Circuit from Streatley via Ridgeway Path and the Fairmile: 10 miles (16 km).
Ascent of 150 yds over 3¼ miles (140 m over 5.1 km) from Streatley to Warren Farm.

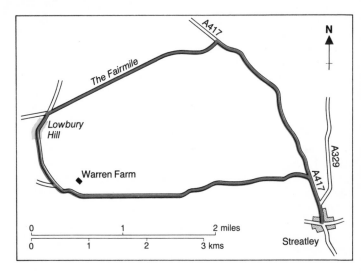

Descent of 38 yds (35 m) in a few hundred yards at Lowbury Hill.
Four and a half miles (7.2 km) on metalled roads.

Leave Streatley travelling north on the A329, turning left on to the A417 and left again at Rectory Lane. Cycle to the end of the lane and on up the unmetalled Ridgeway. After 1½ miles (2.4 km) take the grassy path leading off to the right, at the summit of the first ascent of the Ridgeway and just past Warren Farm.

The route arcs round to the right on the level before dropping swiftly down Lowbury Hill. The surface is firm but uneven chalk: OK in the dry, potentially treacherous in the wet. Shortly after you leave the tree cover, the Fairmile, a broad, grassy path, crosses your route. Turn right here to begin the descent to the main road and Streatley. At the A417 turn right. Streatley is 3 miles away.

Circuit from Aldworth to the Ridgeway via Starveall Farm and back via Streatley Warren: 3½ miles (5.6 km).
No notable ascents or descents.
A mile and a half (2.4 km) on metalled roads.

Leave the village travelling north on a narrow metalled lane leading to the downs. Wide verges leave more space to park here than in the village. After 1½ miles (2.4 km), as you pass

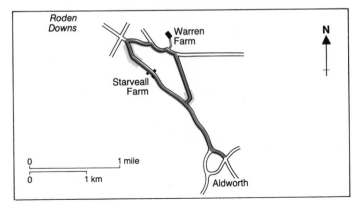

Starveall Farm, the tarmac ends and you are on a dry, wide chalky track leading gently uphill for ½ a mile (0.8 km) towards Roden Downs.

After a few hundred yards the track drops down and joins the Ridgeway. Turn right here. After a ⅓ of a mile, during which you will have climbed 22 yds (20 m over 0.5 km), you will see first a path to the left and then the track to Warren Farm. Take the turning to the right immediately after that. The route runs dead straight and slightly downhill for ½ a mile (0.8 km) before ascending at the same gradient for the same distance.

The path then rises steeply and turns sharp right before meeting the metalled lane to Aldworth. Turn left here. Aldworth is a mile (1.6 km) away.

From Aldworth to Blewbury: 6 miles (9.6 km).
Descent of 90 yds over 1½ miles (80 m over 2.4 km).
Three and a half miles (5.6 km) on metalled road.

Leave the village travelling north on a narrow metalled lane leading to the downs. Wide verges leave more space to park here than in the village. After 1½ miles (2.4 km), as you pass Starveall Farm, the tarmac ends and you are on a dry, wide chalky track leading gently uphill for ½ a mile (0.8 km) towards Roden Downs.

After a few hundred yards the track drops down and joins the Ridgeway. Turn left onto it, then leave it by the second turning on the right, about ½ a mile (0.8 km) on.

The route runs through a clump of trees and then becomes a broad, level path which crosses the Fairmile after a few hundred yards. Gallops appear on both left and right of the track and, after just under 2 miles (3.2 km) the way becomes tarmacked and dips down for the fast, smooth descent into Blewbury, 1½ miles (2.4 km) away.

For an alternative route from Blewbury back to Aldworth turn right at the bottom of the lane onto the A417 and cycle uphill for a mile until, at the crest of a hill, you meet the lane leading to Aston Tirrold on your left. Turn right opposite it onto a lane signposted "The Downs". Now follow the directions in the next section.

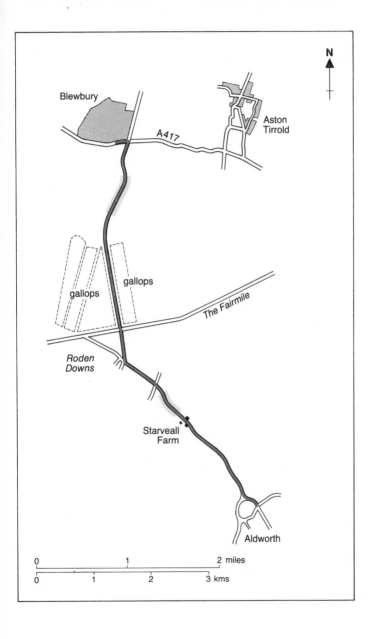

N

Blewbury

Aston
Tirrold

A417

gallops

gallops

The Fairmile

Roden
Downs

Starveall
Farm

Aldworth

0		1		2 miles
0	1	2		3 kms

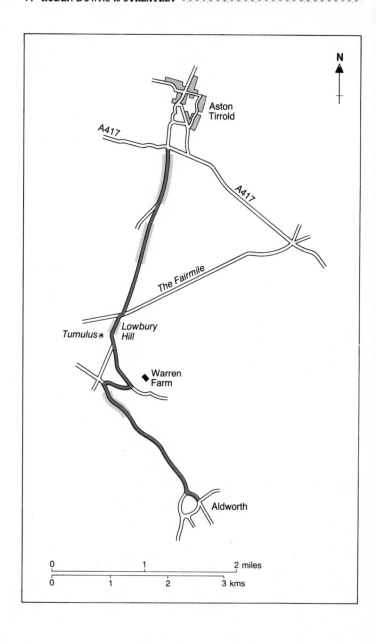

N

Aston
Tirrold

A417

A417

The Fairmile

Tumulus *

Lowbury
Hill

◆ Warren
Farm

Aldworth

0   1   2 miles

0   1   2   3 kms

From the A417 near Aston Tirrold to Aldworth: 5½ miles (8.8 km).
Ascent of 140 yds over 2 miles (130 m over 3.2 km) from the A417 to the Fairmile. Ascent of 40 yds (35 m) in a few hundred yards at Lowbury Hill.
Two and a half miles (4 km) on metalled roads.

The ride begins at a point where the lane signposted to Aston Tirrold leaves the A417. Take the road opposite, signposted to "The Downs". There is room to park just by the junction. The lane leads steeply uphill for ¼ of a mile (0.4 km) and then downhill for the same distance.

At a Y-junction where the tarmac ends take the left fork up a rutted and often muddy incline. After a mile (1.6 km) you reach a crossroads where the Fairmile, a broad, grassy route, crosses your path. Left would take you down to the A417, right leads to the Ridgeway.

Carry straight on up Lowbury Hill along a rutted track climbing steeply through trees. At the Y-junction as the way levels out take the left fork, which is a grassy route and the less distinct of the two, with Warren Farm on the horizon further to your left.

After ¼ of a mile (0.4 km) you meet the Ridgeway, signposted at this point. Turn right, then first left. The path you want here doubles back at a sharp angle. Take care not to miss it. Aldworth is 2 miles (3.2 km) away.

Facilities

GORING AND STREATLEY
Between them, Goring and Streatley have most facilities you will need, including banks, a full range of shops, cafes, restaurants, pubs and hotels. There is a railway station, with trains to Reading, London and Bristol, to the east of Goring.

Accommodation
Miller of Mansfield Hotel, High Street, Goring (0491 872829).
The Swan Diplomat Hotel, Streatley (0491 873737).
The Grange, Manor Road, Goring (0491 872853).
The John Barleycorn, Manor Road, Goring (0491 872509).

Youth Hostel, Hill House, Reading Road, Streatley (0491 872278).
Pub
The Bull, Streatley (0491 872392).
Railway station
Trains to Reading, London Paddington and Bristol (0491 872822).

BLEWBURY
Blewbury Service Station also has a general store selling food, alcohol, and fast-food meals which can be heated up in the shop's microwave. There is a post office in the main street, and a teashop just off the green.
Accommodation
The Load of Mischief (0235 850281).

ALDWORTH
Pub
The Bell Inn (0635 578272).

Tourist information

Reading (0734 566226).